The Best of **NURSERY** educ

Favourite themes

Ages 3-5

▸ **Ourselves**
▸ **Minibeasts**
▸ **Growth**
▸ **Weather**
▸ **Festivals**
▸ **Under the sea**

All the best activities from the UK's leading early years magazine

Editor
Susan Elliott

Designers
Andrea Lewis and Joy Monkhouse

Cover photograph
Ray Moller

Acknowledgement
Qualifications and Curriculum Authority for the use of extracts from the QCA/ DfEE document Curriculum Guidance for the Foundation Stage © 2000 Qualification and Curriculum Authority.

© 2005, Scholastic Ltd

Published by Scholastic Ltd, Villiers House, Clarendon Avenue, Leamington Spa, Warwickshire CV32 5PR.

Visit our website at www.scholastic.co.uk

Printed in Singapore.

2 3 4 5 6 7 8 9 0   6 7 8 9 0 1 2 3 4

British Library Cataloguing-in-Publication Data. A catalogue record for this book is available from the British Library.

ISBN 0-439-96509-8
ISBN 9-780-439-96509-5

Contents

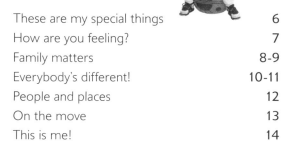
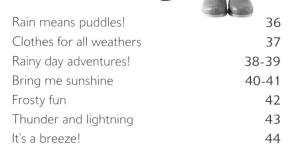
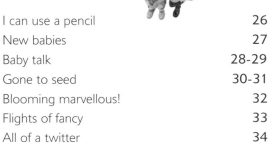

Foreword

By Sue Owen, Director, Early Childhood Unit, National Children's Bureau.

Even the most well qualified, experienced and creative of professionals need a few fresh ideas from time to time.

Most early years practitioners take inspiration from the practical projects and themes provided, in abundance, by magazines aimed at our sector, and *Nursery Education's* are among the best.

A recent study on how early years practitioners access information, conducted by the National Children's Bureau, found that the majority of respondents relied on magazines for up-dates and tips as well as on their colleagues.

This series helpfully pulls together a collection of *Nursery Education's* projects, so you can find them all in one place.

Often the best ideas and projects arise out of children's own interests – many of which are reflected in this collection. The collection offers new ideas (and reminders for some trusted favourites which you may have forgotten) as springboards for your work.

Resources such as this are an ideal addition to team discussions. They can stimulate new thinking as well as bringing the knowledge of a wide range of early years experts to the table.

Thanks to *Nursery Education's* new resource collection, practitioners will now have access to a pool of information from colleagues across the country.

Introduction

If you're a regular subscriber to *Nursery Education*, you'll already appreciate just what a versatile, time-saving resource the magazine is. Each issue contains all you need to deliver a themed project in your setting, plus essential information that enables you to keep up-to-date with current developments in the early years sector.

We've built on this successful formula and made it even better by selecting the very best activities and information from past issues of the magazine, and compiling them into a series of exciting new books.

Each title is packed full of original ideas that are guaranteed to enthuse your children and inspire your staff. In this book, you'll find a selection of cross-curricular activities that will help to develop the children's skills across the six Areas of Learning. Each chapter is based on a favourite early years theme, and in this book we've included activities and action rhymes based on the themes of Ourselves, Minibeasts, Growth, Weather, Festivals and Under the sea.

We've had great fun putting this new set of books together, and we hope you find them to be a valuable addition to your setting! If you would like more information on *Nursery Education*, please visit our website www.scholastic.co.uk, telephone: 0845 850 4411 or see page 64 of this book.

Sarah Sodhi, Editor,
Nursery Education magazine.

Chapter 1
Ourselves

From families to feelings, the games and investigations in this chapter will help children to think not only about themselves but also about their families, friends and immediate environment.

These are my special things

A teddy in my bed at night.
A torch, to beam the brightest light.

My scooter or my trike to ride.
A secret place, where I can hide.

A splashy bath with bubbly foam.
The ones I love, inside my home.

My little dog to run with me,
And granny, coming round to tea.

A holiday with sea and sun.
A party, where we all have fun.

Storytime at nursery school
and feeding ducks around the pool.

My friends who come to play each day.
I like these things a special way.

© Brenda Williams

© Gaynor Berry

Favourite themes

How are you feeling?

Use these activities to help the children talk about their own feelings and those of other people

Be happy!
Stepping Stone: display high levels of involvement in activities (PSED).
Early Learning Goal: be confident to try new activities, initiate ideas and speak in a familiar group (PSED).
Group size: six to eight children.

What you need
Magazines; card; dowelling; sticky tape; scissors; glue; box covered with colourful paper.

What to do
● Ask the children to cut out large pictures of faces from magazines. Make sure that these show a range of facial expressions such as smiling, crying, laughing, bored and angry.
● Stick the pictures on to card and trim carefully around them. Tape a dowelling handle to the back of each card face shape then place the masks in an attractive box.
● In turn, invite the children to choose a mask from the box. Encourage the others in the group to try to describe the feeling that is portrayed by the mask.
● Invite the children to talk about times when they have felt this way and why they felt like that.

© John Fortunato/Soda

Further ideas
● Read *Lucy's Quarrel* by Jennifer Northway (Scholastic). Discuss what happens in the story and the feelings that are generated.

● Make Plasticine figures and create expressions on their faces using sharpened pencils.

Support and extension
Encourage younger children to distinguish between happy faces and sad faces. Older and more able children can look through magazines to find expressions that match those on the 'masks'.

Today I feel...
Stepping Stone: express needs and feelings in appropriate ways (PSED).
Early Learning Goal: have a developing awareness of their own needs, views and feelings and be sensitive to the needs, views and feelings of others (PSED).
Learning objective: to have a developing awareness of their own feelings.
Group size: up to ten children.

What you need
Pictures showing different facial expressions; books about feelings (Wayland's *Your Feelings* series includes *I'm bored, I'm happy, I'm worried* and *I'm lonely*).

What to do
● Sit in a circle on the floor. Read a book about feelings and discuss the content with the group.
● Share the pictures of different facial expressions. Invite the children to discuss. Next, ask how each person is feeling and why they may be feeling like that.
● Point to the picture as you say 'I am like this person today because I feel...' sad, angry, scared, hurt, happy and so on.
● Invite one child to take the picture and point to the person that they feel like, then encourage them to pass it to the next child so that they can do the same. Pass the picture around the circle until everyone has had an opportunity to talk about how they feel. Do not force anyone to take part if they do not want to do so.
● During another session, invite the children to extend their responses to say how they feel and why they feel like that, if they wish.

Support and extension
Ask younger children to look for the happy and sad people in the picture. When the children become more confident at expressing their feelings use the picture to allow them to express how they feel about conflict within the group.

Home links
● Ask carers to encourage children to express their feelings outside the group situation.

● Ask for donations of old magazines and family supplements.

Kevin Kelman is a deputy headteacher and writer.

Family matters

Develop skills in language and literacy as you focus on families

Jenny jumps!

Stepping Stone: begin to recognise some simple words (CLL).

Early Learning Goal: read a range of familiar and common words and simple sentences independently (CLL).

Group size: any size.

What you need

Large, empty floor space; two large cubes made from thick cardboard (each side measuring approximately 20cm by 20cm). On one cube draw the head and shoulders of family members such as 'daddy', 'cousin', 'grandson', and label each picture. On the other cube draw and label a simple activity such as 'swims' or 'cooks'.

© Gaynor Berry

What to do

● Show the children the cubes and together read each of the words.

● Throw the dice with the people on. Read the word accompanying the picture on the uppermost side of the dice. Next, throw the activities dice. Again, read the word that accompanies the picture. Encourage the children to help you put the two words together to make a simple sentence, for example, 'Grandma swims'.

● Invite the children to take turns to throw both dice and to read aloud the words on each.

Support and extension

Use simple words for younger children. Make an extra dice for older children with drawings of places where each activity could be happening, such as the lounge or the garden. Encourage the children to throw each dice in order to make a sentence.

Further ideas

● Role-play family situations using puppets of family members.

● Make a 'My family does...' book. Add the children's drawings of something that their family does together, with appropriate captions.

In my photograph album

Stepping Stone: use talk to connect ideas (CLL).

Early Learning Goal: to use language to recreate roles and experiences (CLL).

Group size: large or small groups.

What you need

Large, empty floor space.

What to do

● Sit together on the floor in a large circle.

● Talk about the photographs that you might find in a photograph album. Who might you see in the photographs?

● Explain that you are going to play a game, and you would like the children to think of people that they would like to put photographs of in their album, such as 'Mummy' or 'Uncle Joe'.

● Begin by saying, 'In my photograph album there is a picture of... (my cousin)'. The next child should say, 'In my photograph album there is a picture of (Mrs Cook's) cousin and... (my mummy)'.

● Continue around the circle, helping the children to add one more person to the photograph album each time.

Support and extension

Encourage younger children to include just one person in their sentence and not try to list the previous people. Invite older children to think of something that each person in the album could be doing in the photograph.

Home links

● Make a group recipe book. Ask families to write down their favourite recipe. Laminate the recipes and leave them in the role-play area for the children to 'read'.

Family tree

Stepping Stone: talk activities through, reflecting and modifying what they are doing (CLL).

Early Learning Goal: use talk to organize, sequence and clarify thinking, ideas and events (CLL).

Group size: small groups.

What you need

Tree shape cut from brown and green card, stuck on to A1 card; white paper (15cm by 15cm); drawing and writing materials; glue.

What to do

● Invite the children to think of lots of different people that can be in a family, such as grandparents, cousins, brothers and sisters.
● Scribe a name for each person on separate pieces of white paper.
● Give each child a piece of paper with a name on it and ask them to draw an appropriate picture for the word.
● Show the tree shape that you made earlier and encourage the children to arrange the pictures on the tree so that the oldest person is at the top of the tree and the youngest is at the bottom near the trunk.
● Encourage discussion as the children talk about the ages of the different people and work out

© John Fortunato/Soda

where to place them on the tree.
● Help the children to glue the pictures in place on the shape.

Support and extension

Invite younger children to name the family members that they see regularly. Ask older children to talk about their reasons for the placing of the pictures.

My name means...

Stepping Stone: distinguish one sound from another (CLL).

Early Learning Goal: link sounds to letters, naming and sounding the letters of the alphabet (CLL).

Group size: three or four children.

What you need

Book of children's names, such as *15,000+ Baby Names* by Bruce Lansky (Meadowbrook Press); alphabet poster or frieze; white A4 paper; pen.

What to do

● Find the page in the book on which each child's name appears. On a sheet of A4 paper, write down the child's name, together with a couple of names that appear before and after their name in the book. Include the meanings of the names. Copy the sheets so that each child has a copy of each name sheet.
● Talk about how babies are named. Explain that many names have a meaning. Read one of the names and its meaning from a photocopied sheet.
● Tell the children that you want to find out what the name of each child in the group means, and hand out the photocopied sheets for just one of the children's names.

● Together, choose one of the names, spelling out the word if necessary and reminding the children about alphabetical order. As a group, read through the meaning together.
● Repeat for the rest of the children's names.

Support and extension

For younger children, enlarge the text on the photocopier and provide just one or two other names on each photocopy. Encourage older children to work more independently to find the relevant names.

© Gaynor Berry

Lorraine Gale is a teacher and writer.

Everybody's different

These practical activities provide opportunities to develop skills in counting and comparing, and to develop mathematical language

Body shapes
Stepping Stone: show an interest in shape and space by playing with shapes or making arrangements with objects (MD).
Early Learning Goal: use language to describe the shape and size of solid and flat objects; to recreate simple patterns (MD).
Group size: small groups or whole group.

What you need
Large, open space; large 2-D circle, square and triangle; skittles or free-standing posts.

What to do
● Using the 2-D shapes, help the children to find and identify circles, squares and triangles around your setting.
● Ask them to work with their friends and use their arms, legs or whole bodies to form circles, squares or triangles. Encourage them to try different ways to make the shapes. Can they form the shape lying on the ground and standing up?
● Once they have made their shapes, challenge them to walk around the area to form a circle, square or a triangle. Invite a child who does it correctly to be a leader for others to follow. If they have difficulties, place the skittles in the required shape for them to march around.

Support and extension
Younger children can focus on making long, tall shapes or short, wide shapes. Encourage appropriate

language to describe the ways that they are using their bodies. Challenge older children to work together to form a pattern of body shapes, for example, circle, square, triangle, circle and so on. Encourage individuals to join the line and continue the pattern.

© James Levin/Soda

Further ideas
● Weigh the children using bathroom scales. Compare the different weights.

● Measure distances around your setting in footprints or handspans. Record your findings.

This is our group!
Stepping Stone: use mathematical language in play (MD).
Early Learning Goal: say and use number names in familiar contexts. (MD)
Group size: whole group.

What you need
Lively music; music-playing facilities; safe, open area.

What to do
● Play the music and encourage the children to dance about the open space. When you stop the music, challenge the children to form two lines according to various criteria, for example: boys/girls; wearing jumpers/not wearing jumpers; aged four/aged five; wearing trainers/wearing shoes.
● Compare the length of the lines. Which is

longest/shortest? How many children in each line? How many more in the longer line? Who is behind (Samir)? In front of (Adam)?
● Start the music again. This time, when you stop the music, call out a number between two and five. Challenge the children to form a group of that number and then sit down.
● Count the groups. How many children are left over? How many more would they need to form another group? To ensure that the left-over children form a group next time, allow them to stay together.

Support and extension
Let younger children sort dolls according to different criteria. Older children can form groups of larger numbers, beyond five. When they are confident, use number cards instead of calling out the numbers.

Home links
● Develop children's understanding of mathematical language of height and weight by asking carers to compare changes in clothes sizes. For example, 'these jeans are too short – you must have grown taller!'.

Favourite themes

Who is the tallest?

Stepping Stone: order two items by length or height (MD).

Early Learning Goal: use developing mathematical ideas and methods to solve practical problems (MD).

Group size: six to eight children.

What you need
Long, narrow strips of paper; colouring and writing materials.

What to do
● Ask one child to stand at the front. In turn invite the rest of the children to stand next to the first child. Compare heights, and then sort the children into groups according to who is taller/ shorter. How many children are taller? How many are shorter?

● Invite three children to sort themselves in order of height. When they have done this successfully, invite the whole group to sort themselves in height order. Discuss the order of the children. Is Daniel taller than Sareeta? Who is shorter than Lewis?

● Cut a strip of paper for each child that is the same length as their height. Let them colour the strips in and write their names on them. Allow the children to compare their own strips with each others', discussing the comparisons. For example 'Mine is longer, so I am taller than you!' Mount

the strips in size order and discuss the display. Who is tallest? Who is shortest?

Support and extension
Introduce younger children to using their bodies as non-standard units of measurement. What can they find that is the same length as their foot or their handspan? Invite older children to help you to caption the display, for example, 'Rajan is tallest, so his strip is first. Emma is shortest, so her strip is last'.

Watch me!

Stepping Stone: show an interest in numbers and counting (MD).

Early Learning Goal: say and use number names in order in familiar contexts (MD).

Group size: small groups.

What you need
Large open space; skittles or free-standing obstacles.

What to do
● Place two skittles a short distance apart. How many strides would the children need to take to cover the distance? Invite them to guess before letting one child try out their guesses. Did they take more or less strides? How many more/less?

● Next, try jumps or hops. Count together as one child tries out the group's estimate.

● Change the position of the skittles. Guess and then test the guesses again. Were the children correct this time?

● Invite the children to make up movement patterns, for example, two strides, three hops, two strides and so on. Let them demonstrate their pattern for the others to copy.

Support and extension
Work with just two or three younger children and do the striding/hopping together. Older children can see who can move the furthest distance in ten strides or ten hops. What about 20 strides/hops?

Barbara Garrad is an early years educationist and freelance writer.

People and places

Help the children to think carefully about their immediate environment and to reflect on past events

On my way

Stepping Stone: comment and ask questions about where they live (KUW).
Early Learning Goal: observe, find out about and identify features in the place they live and the natural world (KUW).
Group size: four children.

What you need

Large sheets of paper; drawing materials; whiteboard and pens.

Preparation

Ask carers for information on where the children live and their routes to the setting.

What to do

● Begin by telling the children how you got to your setting today. List some of the buildings or landmarks that you passed and transport you used.
● On the whiteboard, draw a picture map of your journey, marking significant buildings such as the Post Office or Police Station. Include yourself on or in your mode of transport.
● Ask the children to think about how they got to your setting today. In turn, let them share their ideas as they recall things about their journey and mode of transport.
● Invite the children to draw their own picture map of their journey. Support them by asking about the buildings that they pass and any signs or objects that help them to recognize the purpose of the buildings.

Support and extension

Make picture flash cards with younger children to show some of the places and buildings that they pass. Put them in order to make a picture story.
Invite older children to make models of the buildings using junk materials and paints. Place them in order on the floor to make a 3-D picture story.

© James Levin/Soda

Further ideas

● Go for a walk in the locality to look at the buildings and to observe their purpose. Visit the Post Office to buy stamps or post letters.

I like to...

Stepping Stone: remember and talk about significant things that have happened to them (KUW).
Early Learning Goal: find out about past and present events in their own lives (KUW).
Group size: up to eight children.

What you need

A special object (such as a shell) for the children to hold to indicate the 'speaker'.

Preparation

Ask the children to sit in a circle and to think carefully about some of the things that they like to do with their families at weekends or in the evenings.

What to do

● Explain that you would like to hear about some of the activities that the children enjoy at home.
● Begin by holding the shell yourself and telling the children about your weekend. If appropriate, mention any special clothing that you wore, other people that were with you and any interesting places that you went to.
● Pass the shell to the child on your right and ask questions to find out about some of the things that he or she likes to do. Encourage the children to listen carefully to each other. All children who wish to speak should have the opportunity, but if they would rather not speak, then they should pass the shell to the next person.

Support and extension

Help younger children to remember their news by asking appropriate questions. Invite older children to bring in items from home to talk about as they recall their news.

Home links

● Make a display of photographs and other special objects that the children bring in from home. Help each child to add a label describing their photograph or object.

Gill Walton is a nursery teacher.

On the move

Have fun finding out how our bodies move, and create some watery footprint patterns with these activities

Crooked or straight?

Stepping Stone: manage body to create intended movements (PD).
Early Learning Goal: move with control and coordination (PD).
Group size: whole group.

What you need

Bare feet; a large open area.

What to do

● Gather the group together and talk about how our muscles need to be warm before they can work properly. Warm up by stretching and shrinking slowly, using bodies to make tall, small, wide and narrow shapes before again drawing the group together.
● Ask the children to walk around the room using all of the available space until you signal them to stop.
● Repeat, this time asking the children to walk sometimes backwards or sideways, but always looking where they are going. Ask them to think about what their arms and legs are doing. Are they bent or straight? Can they walk with really bent arms and really straight legs?
● Repeat the exercise walking on hands and feet. Encourage the children to move in all directions and with all combinations of bent or straight limbs.
● Finish by asking the children to choose whether to be completely bent or completely straight and trying to stay that way as they walk back to put on their socks and shoes!

© James Levin/Soda

Support and extension

Encourage younger children to join in by doing so yourself. Encourage them to copy your actions if they prefer. Help older children to extend their movements by pointing or flexing their wrists and ankles as well as knees and elbows.

Further ideas

● Use paint and huge sheets of paper to make permanent footprint patterns.

● Practise performing everyday activities in an unusual way, for example, sitting down without bending your legs or drawing without using your hands.

Footprints

Stepping Stone: experiment with different ways of moving (PD).
Early Learning Goal: move with confidence, imagination and in safety (PD).
Group size: up to eight children.

What you need

Shallow trays of water; wellington boots; dry, safe outdoor paved area.

What to do

● Start the activity by inviting the children to walk around the area, sometimes taking long strides and sometimes short ones.
● Encourage them to think of different ways of getting around on their feet, for example, hopping, skipping or jumping. What patterns are they making with their feet? Suggest that it might be

fun to see some feet patterns.
● Space out the trays of water in the area. Talk about what the water might be for and lead the group to discover that wet shoes will leave a trail of footprints.
● Let the children move freely around the area, carefully stepping into any trays that they come to and trying to create as many different patterns as they can.
● Stop occasionally to inspect an interesting pattern and ask the children how it might have been created and whether they can recreate it themselves.

Support and extension

Allow younger children time to merely enjoy treading in the water and making footprints. Encourage older children to think about the angles at which they place their feet as well as where they place them on the ground.

Home links

● Ask parents and carers to play 'Follow the leader' with their children to practise different ways of moving.

Barbara J Leach is former head of a 4+ Unit in Leicestershire.

This is me!

Try your hand at colour mixing and investigate shadow shapes with these creative ideas

Profile portraits
Stepping Stone: use their bodies to explore texture and space (CD).
Early Learning Goal: explore shape, form and space in two or three dimensions (CD).
Group size: small groups.

What you need
Overhead projector or very bright desk light; A2 white paper; black pencils or felt-tipped pens; safety scissors; masking tape.

What to do
● Tape a sheet of paper to the wall at a child's head height. Ask a child to stand in front of the paper, and line up the OHP or light so that it casts a shadow of the child's head and shoulders on the paper. Use masking tape to mark the position where the children should stand.
● Invite the children to tell you about their faces. Their observations may include facial features and the colour of their eyes or hair.
● Explain that a side view of the face is called a 'profile'. Ask a child to stand sideways between the paper and the OHP, and demonstrate how to draw around the shadow cast on the paper using a pencil or felt-tipped pen.
● Remove the drawing and compare the child's profile to your drawing. Tape a clean sheet of paper to the wall.

© Dan Howell/Soda

● Let the children work in pairs, taking turns to cast shadows and draw around each other's profiles. Provide a safe, stable surface to stand on if necessary.
● Mount your shadow pictures to make a 'Profile portrait gallery'.

Support and extension
Ask younger children just to outline the facial features of each shadow. Older children could try to guess the owner of each shadow profile.

Colour me
Stepping Stone: try to capture experiences and responses with paint (CD).
Early Learning Goal: express and communicate their ideas, thoughts and feelings by using a widening range of materials (CD).
Group size: small groups.

What you need
Selection of paint charts; thick white A4 paper; painting equipment and resources including paints in primary colours.

What to do
● Invite the children to look at their hands. What colour are they? Discuss the differences between skin tones and colours.
● Look at the paint charts and talk about the different colours.

● Work together to try to find colours on the paint charts that match the children's skin colours.
● Give each child some paper and painting materials. Invite the children to mix the paints to try to make colours that match as closely as possible to the colours that you identified on the paint charts. Encourage them to fill their sheet of paper with paint.
● When dry, invite the children to place their hand on their painting and to draw around the outline. Trim the hand shapes and label with the children's names then display on a wall to make a circle of hands.

Support and extension
Support younger children by suggesting colours to add to make the correct shade. Encourage older children to experiment with lightening and darkening the colours to try to create the same shade as on the paint chart.

Further ideas
● Cut out the shadow pictures and mount on black paper to make silhouettes.

● Blindfold a child and invite them to carefully feel another child's face and try to guess their identity.

Home links
● Let each child make a clay face which they can paint and take home.

Lorraine Gale is a teacher and writer.

Chapter 2
Minibeasts

Take a closer look at the creepy crawlies that we share our world with using the fun activities in this chapter. Ideas include counting games based on spotty minibeasts and instructions for growing your own hairy caterpillars!

The minibeast feast

Creep like a caterpillar   *(Mime the actions of the different minibeasts.)*
Buzz like a bee
March like an ant
Down the old oak tree.

Fly like a ladybird   *(Pretend to fly and flutter.)*
Or a butterfly
Weave like spiders   *(Skip around, linking arms with different partners.)*
On a branch up high.

Hide like a beetle   *(Curl up, hiding face.)*
Slither like a snail
Run like a centipede   *(Slither slowly and then run quickly.)*
Down the trail.

Come to the party   *(Join hands to form a circle.)*
Every minibeast
Today is the day   *(Dance round and round.)*
Of the minibeast feast!

© Brenda Williams

Spinning spiders

Provide opportunities for children to experience a sense of achievement with these ideas based on spiders

We can do it!

Stepping Stone: demonstrate a sense of pride in own achievement (PSED).
Early Learning Goal: dress and undress independently (PSED).
Group size: up to eight children.

What you need
The children's coats.

What to do
● Begin by singing the rhyme 'Incy Wincy Spider' (Traditional). Talk through the rhyme together. Why did Incy climb up the spout again? Help the children to understand the meaning of perseverance and sticking at a task until they have mastered it.
● Ask the children to give examples of times when they have had to persevere. Offer suggestions, for example, they may have spilled their drink many times before they were able to drink with confidence from a cup without a lid.
● Reinforce the idea by telling the children a simplified version of the legend of Robert the Bruce, the Scottish leader, who hid from his pursuers in a cave, feeling that all his battles were lost. He spotted a spider that was having difficulty in securing its web to the roof of the cave. Although the spider failed several times, it kept on trying, and on its seventh attempt it was successful. Robert the Bruce took this to be a good sign and decided to keep trying.
● Put the idea into practice by inviting the children to put on and do up their own coats.
● Plan time to help the children practise this task. Encourage them to take the initiative, stepping in only when a child is really struggling. Give lots of praise for any small achievement.

Support and extension
Let younger children practise with a tabard apron before attempting a coat. Involve older children who have already mastered dressing skills in assisting those still practising it.

© Photodisc Inc.

Home links
● Share the children's achievements with parents. Let the children demonstrate that they can put on their coat unaided.

● Ask parents to help the children find spiders' webs at home.

Web watch

Stepping Stone: have a strong exploratory impulse (PSED).
Early Learning Goal: continue to be interested, excited and motivated to learn (PSED).
Group size: up to eight children.

What you need
Magnifying glasses; copy of *The Very Busy Spider* by Eric Carle (Hamish Hamilton).

What to do
● Read the story of *The Very Busy Spider* and talk about the different stages that the spider goes through to build a web.
● Why do spiders build webs? Discuss how the spiders use their webs to catch insects for food.

● Give the children magnifying glasses and ask them to look in corners and areas of the room where people often forget to dust, searching for webs. When the children find a web, make sure it is unoccupied and encourage them to look closely at the intricate pattern.
● Encourage them to gently touch the web and to describe what it feels like. Is it sticky? Can anyone tell you why it needs to be sticky?

Support and extension
Help younger children by directing them to areas where the webs might be. Be sensitive to any of the children's fears about spiders. Provide older children with thread, wool and string and invite them to build giant webs by threading the resources around chair legs.

Further ideas
● Look outdoors for different-shaped webs. A south-facing wall can house many spiders and funnel-shaped webs.

Lorraine Frankish
is an early years tutor and NVQ Assessor.

Creative creatures

Enjoy playing with words and sounds with these exciting activities about lots of different minibeasts!

Glow little glow-worm, glow!

Stepping Stone: continue a rhyming string (CLL).
Early Learning Goal: hear and say initial and final sounds in words, and short vowel sounds within words (CLL).
Group size: up to ten children.

What you need
A flip chart.

What to do
● Explain that a glow-worm is a kind of beetle. The female glows at night to attract the male to her.

● Invite the children to think of other things that 'glow' in the dark such as lighthouses, candles, torches and phosphorescent star stickers.
● Play with the word 'glow'. Write on the flip chart words that the children suggest that rhyme with this sound, for example, 'low', 'slow', 'grow', 'throw', 'so', 'no', 'blow', 'snow' and 'go'.
● Have fun making up nonsense rhymes with the children using as many of these words as possible, starting with 'Glow little glow-worm, glow! Go slow little glow-worm, slow'.
● Try the same idea using the words of other things that glow, such as 'Grow lighthouse grow!' or 'Snow candle, snow!'.
● Challenge the children to make up their own simple nonsense rhyme using some of their ideas.

Support and extension
Explain to younger children that in nonsense rhymes, you can say silly things! Invite older children to think of words that rhyme with snail, for example, 'pale snail' and 'snail in a gale'. Encourage them to draw pictures of their own ideas.

Home links
● Suggest that the children collect small toy minibeasts and create stories about them.

● Ask parents to help their children find minibeasts and later tell another adult about them.

Spider stories

Stepping Stone: know information can be relayed in the form of print (CLL).
Early Learning Goals: know that print carries meaning; read a range of familiar and common words and simple sentences independently (CLL).
Group size: up to ten children.

What you need
Black and red sugar paper; white chalk; black marker pen; flip chart; two white cardboard circles (approximately 90cm diameter); pictures of spiders.

What to do
● Help the children to cut a large spider's body from black sugar paper, approximately 20cm across. Cut eight wide legs, each approximately 35cm long, and attach to the spider's body.
● Discuss the spider pictures together. Ask the children to tell you what they know about spiders.

● Record the children's comments about the spiders on the flip chart in simple sentences, for example, 'spiders have eight legs'; 'spiders live in a web' and so on. Read each comment together as you write it.
● Help the children to glue the large spider's body on to a card circle. Choose eight appropriate comments to write on to the legs of the spider, using white chalk.
● Show the children how to turn the circle slowly and read the sentences on each leg, like a book.
● Make another spider in red, with black writing. This time ask the children to name the spider and make up a simple story. For example: My name is Sammy. I live in a cupboard...' and so on.

Support and extension
Pin the cardboard circles to a display board to facilitate turning for younger children. Invite older children to make up their own spider stories.

Further ideas
● Observe minibeasts in a magnifying 'bug-cup'. Invite the children to describe them and record their comments on minibeast-shaped paper.

● Make two large soft spiders from black tights, and ask the children to make up conversations between them.

Brenda Williams
is an early years specialist and freelance writer.

Caterpillar creep

Stepping Stone: begin to form recognisable letters (CLL).
Early Learning Goal: use a pencil and hold it effectively to form recognisable letters, most of which are correctly formed (CLL).
Group size: five children.

What you need
Six strips of paper measuring 15cm by 40cm; chubby pencils.

What to do
● On one strip of paper, draw a simple coloured drawing of a caterpillar, looking to the right and forming three clear humps as it wriggles along.
● Mark the other strips on the long side of the paper with a green dot 5cm from the left, and then three plain pencil dots at 10cm intervals (four dots altogether).
● Show the children your picture of a caterpillar, and ask them to make their own by starting at the green dot and drawing a hump to the next dot and then another to the next and so on.
● Demonstrate to the children how to hold their pencil and where to start. Encourage them to complete all three humps without taking their pencil off the paper.

© Corel

● Invite the children to draw a body around the humps to create a caterpillar like yours and to colour it in.

Support and extension
Use larger pieces of paper for younger children to draw the caterpillar with a thick crayon. Extend the length of the paper for older children to draw four humps in a row, and then five.

Journey of a butterfly

Stepping Stone: hear and say the initial sound in words and know which letters represent some of the words (CLL).
Early Learning Goals: hear and say initial sounds in words; link sounds to letters (CLL).
Group size: whole group initially; five children for the activity.

What you need
Cardboard; crayons; scissors; green and brown display paper; display board; Blu-Tack.

What to do
● Discuss where the children have seen butterflies. If possible, go outside and look for butterflies around your settting or the local area.
● Back inside, involve the children in making and colouring cardboard cut-outs of things that a butterfly might encounter on a journey around the garden, ensure that each has a different initial sound, such as 'apple', 'bucket' and 'cabbage'.

© Rebecca Finn

● Cover the display board with green backing paper to represent grass. At child height, add a winding path, cut from brown backing paper. Draw the outline of each of the cardboard cut-outs along the path and write the initial letter of each object inside the outline. Attach the cardboard cut-outs to one side of the board with Blu-Tack.
● Invite the children to start the trail at different places each day, using the outlines to help them identify the initial sound and read the letter inside. challenge the children to find the object among the selection of cut-outs and attach it to the correct outline on the display board with Blu-Tack.

Support and extension
Help younger children to trace the shape of the letters displayed with their finger, saying its sound as they do so. Suggest that older children draw similar trails for house spiders and talk about them to the rest of group.

Minibeast maths

Focus on a range of maths skills as you find out about the features of different minibeasts

Ladybird spots

Stepping Stone: select the correct numeral to represent 1 to 5, then 1 to 9, objects (MD).
Early Learning Goal: recognise numerals 1 to 9 (MD).
Group size: small groups.

What you need

Red and green card; scissors; black marker pens; numbered or dotted dice.

What to do

● Cut 12 ovals from the red card and explain that these represent ladybirds. Share them out and ask the children to use a black marker to draw up to six spots on each ladybird.
● Cut a large leaf outline from green card and lay it on the floor. Ask the children to sit around it.
● Show the children a dice and point to the different dots or numbers. Encourage them to say the numbers out loud and hold up the corresponding number of fingers.
● Invite the children to take turns to throw the dice. If it shows, for example, three dots (or number 3), that child should choose a ladybird showing three spots and pass the dice on.

© Corel

● If there are no ladybirds with three spots, the child misses that turn. Continue playing until all the ladybirds have flown away and the leaf is bare.

Support and extension

Write the corresponding number on to each ladybird alongside the spots to help younger children. Encourage older children to add the total number of spots on their ladybirds to see who has the highest score.

Home links
● Encourage parents to explore the number eight with their child. Ask them to go on a 'number eight hunt' at home, or help their child sort objects into groups of eight.

Further ideas
● Sort plastic minibeasts into hoops. Encourage the children to suggest how the creatures should be sorted, for example, by colour or number of wings.

● Create a 'patternpillar' number line, starting with a short caterpillar with one body segment, then longer caterpillars, up to ten. Invite the children to number the parts and display the patternpillar in your maths area.

● Count the legs on the creatures on the A3 poster in this issue.

Allison Hedley
is a nursery nurse and Degree student at Sunderland University.

Caterpillar patterns

Stepping Stone: show an interest in shape and space by playing with shapes or making arrangements with objects (MD).
Early Learning Goal: talk about, recognise and recreate simple patterns (MD).
Group size: small groups.

What you need

Colouring materials; scissors; A4 paper; pictures of caterpillars.

Preparation

On a sheet of A4 paper draw four caterpillars, each with a different number of body serctions (up to ten) and each a different length. Photocopy one sheet for each child.

What to do

● Look at the caterpillar pictures together. Notice that they have long bodies and lots of tiny legs.

● Give each child a photocopied sheet. Count how many body segments there are on each caterpillar. Which has the most segments? Which has the fewest?
● Demonstrate how to colour one of the caterpillar's body segments using a recurring pattern, for example, blue, red, yellow, blue, red, yellow. Encourage the children to create their own recurring pattern. What colours will they use, and in what order? Will all the caterpillars on their sheet have the same pattern?
● Once the children have coloured in their caterpillars, talk about the colours that they chose. Which colour was used the most?

Support and extension

Let younger children use just two or three primary colours. Invite older children to cut their caterpillars into segments and add and take away to make their caterpillars grow and shrink.

Who's hiding?
Stepping Stone: recognise groups with one, two or three objects (MD).
Early Learning Goal: use developing mathematical ideas and methods to solve practical problems (MD).
Group size: small groups.

What you need
White paper; colouring materials; scissors; large stones; eight simple minibeast outlines drawn on to paper; open area (inside or out).

What to do
● Copy the sheet of minibeast outlines twice, so that you have two sets of identical minibeasts.
● Invite the children to colour in the minibeasts, and encourage them to concentrate so that each 'pair' looks the same. Help the children to cut the minibeasts out.
● Invite the children to help you arrange the large stones on the ground outside or indoors. Talk about how minibeasts like to live under stones for warmth, shelter and food.
● Hide the paper minibeasts in a random order under the stones. Encourage the children to take turns to lift up two stones at a time. If the two creatures underneath do not match, put the stones back. If they do, the child keeps the matching pair.
● See who can collect the most minibeast pairs.

Support and extension
Limit the number of stones and minibeasts for younger children. Add a greater variety of minibeasts for older children and a few cut-out flowers that do not match.

Number eight spider
Stepping Stones: recognise numerals 1 to 5, then 1 to 9; count out up to six objects from a larger group (MD).
Early Learning Goal: recognise numerals 1 to 9 (MD).
Group size: whole group.

What you need
Black paper or card (A4 size – cut a couple of sheets into strips lengthwise to make eight 'legs'); circular 'spot' stickers; pictures of real spiders; scissors; white chalk or crayon; orange paper; black marker pen.

What to do
● Cut out a large number eight from a piece of black A4 paper or card. Ask the children to name the number. Can they hold up eight fingers?
● Explain that this large number eight is the spider's body. Use white crayon or chalk to add facial features. How many eyes will the spider need? Look at pictures of real spiders to guide you.
● How many legs does a spider have? Invite individual children to fold the strips of black paper into concertina shapes to make legs for the spider.
● Invite another group of children to cut out eight large orange circles for feet. Glue the feet to the legs and the legs to the body.
● Help the children to count and label each foot from one to eight using the stickers.

Support and extension
Let younger children count and label the legs on a toy spider. Jumble up the spiders' legs for older children. Encourage them to sort them into numerical order before attaching them to the spider.

Bug patrol

Enjoy hunting for evidence of minibeasts around your setting with these fun activities

Feeding time

Stepping Stone: examine objects and living things to find out more about them (KUW).

Early Learning Goal: find out about, and identify, some features of living things they observe (KUW).

Group size: three children.

What you need:

Pictures of butterflies feeding (*Minibeasts* by Lynn Huggins-Cooper, *First Hand Science* series, Franklin Watts, contains useful pictures); party blower; strips of card long enough to fit around a child's head; sticky tape; craft straws; clean drinking straws; polystyrene craft balls; orange juice; beakers; large card flower shape; PVA glue.

What to do

- Check for food allergies and dietary requirements.
- Look at the pictures with the children and notice the butterflies' long tongues. Explain that the butterflies drink nectar from deep in flowers. Their tongues are hollow, just like a straw.
- Talk about the differences between our tongues and butterfly tongues. Show the children a party blower unfurling like a butterfly tongue, and explain that butterflies roll up their tongues when they have finished feeding.
- Involve the children in making headbands from strips of card. Stick on halved polystyrene balls for eyes and add straw antennae.
- Half-fill three beakers with orange juice and put them in the centre of a simple cut out of a flower shape. Explain that the orange is the 'nectar' in the centre of the flower.
- Give each child a drinking straw and invite them to drink the 'nectar' like the butterflies.

Support and extension

Help younger children to make their headgear. Let older children add extra detail to their headgear, for example, making moths with feathered antennae.

Insect inspectors

Stepping Stone: comment and ask questions about where they live and the natural world (KUW).

Early Learning Goal: observe, find out about and identify features in the place they live and the natural world (KUW).

Group size: six children.

What you need

Magnifiers; lettuce or cabbage leaf showing holes caused by slug damage (if necessary, 'manufacture' this); paper; pencils; information books about bugs.

What to do

- Show the children the holey leaf. Tell them that something has damaged the plants in your garden! What do they think it could be? If necessary, guide them towards slugs/snails.
- Ask the children what bugs they think live in and around your setting. How do they know? Have they seen them? Have they seen evidence?
- Explain that you are going to be 'Insect inspectors', looking for clues that tell you there are bugs around!
- Go outside and look for clues such as holes in leaves, slime trails, wood gnawed by wasps, webs and tiny black specks of frass (bug droppings), not forgetting the bugs themselves.
- Prompt the children to suggest which creature left the clue.
- Back inside, encourage the children to record their findings by drawing pictures of the evidence and the bug that left it on sheets of paper.

Support and extension

Point out the 'evidence' to younger children and prompt them with questions such as 'Who made this hole? They must have been able to slide up the side of the plant pot...'. Encourage older children to look at information books about bugs to find other clues to search for such as insect exoskeletons or egg cases.

Home links

- Ask parents to help their children become 'Insect inspectors' at home. Can they find different bugs to those found at your setting?

Further ideas

- Make colourful paper wings to wear with the butterfly headbands. Add string loops to go over the arms to keep them in place.

- Make a lift-the-flap 'Bug clues' frieze with a slug under a holey leaf, a snail under a glittery snail trail and so on.

Lynn Huggins-Cooper is a children's author and PGCE science/DT lecturer.

Keep on moving

Enjoy these lively minibeast movement ideas to develop gross motor skills

Darting dragonflies

Stepping Stone: manage body to create intended movements (PD).
Early Learning Goal: move with control and co-ordination (PD).
Group size: whole group.

What you need

Books or videos showing dragonflies emerging, such as *Minibeasts* by Lynn Huggins-Cooper (*First Hand Science* series, Franklin Watts).

What to do

● Begin by looking at the books or videos to find out about the life cycle of a dragonfly.
● Notice how the dragonfly moves at different stages of its life.
● Tell the children that they are going to pretend to be dragonflies.
● Move with them as you talk through the different stages of the dragonfly's life.
● Explain that the baby dragonfly (larva) is a fierce hunter. It zooms around the pond, squirting water from its back to escape from predators! It grabs and eats tadpoles and even tiny fish.
● Then the dragonfly larva gets tired and settles down to sleep in a chrysalis.

● Eventually, the dragonfly pushes its way out of the chrysalis. It stretches out its wings to dry, fluttering them lightly.
● Finally, the dragonfly flies off, zooming about and hovering over the water as a glittering adult.

Support and extension

Work with smaller groups of younger children and model movements for them to copy. Encourage older children to make up new sequences for other creatures' life cycles, such as frog or butterfly.

RLPA/J Van Arkel/Foto Natura

Home links
● Provide a copy of the poem for the children to share at home with their parents. Ask parents to find some suitable music to accompany it.

Creepy-crawlies

Stepping Stones: move spontaneously within available space; move freely with pleasure and confidence (PD).
Early Learning Goal: move with confidence, imagination and in safety (PD).
Group size: whole group.

What you need

CD player or tape recorder; CD or tape of nature sounds (such as *English Country Dawn* or *Summer Sounds*, both available from SpaceKraft Ltd, tel: 01274-581007); the poem 'Minibeasts moving!' (right); open space.

What to do

● Play the CD or tape as background 'mood music'.
● Encourage the children to imagine that they are in a garden full of minibeasts. Can they name any? How would the different minibeasts move?
● Read the poem 'Minibeasts moving!'.
● Ask the children to suggest ways to put actions to the words, for example, batting their heads to ward off niggling gnats or scurrying like a spider.
● Invite the children to pretend to be their chosen minibeast. Continue for a short while, encouraging the children to choose a different minibeast to imitate on your signal.
● End by sitting quietly and listening to the music.

Support and extension

Let younger children copy your suggested movements. Older children can suggest and model movements for others to copy.

Minibeasts moving!

Slugs slide
Snails glide

Spiders scurry
Wasps hurry

Caterpillars creep
Grasshoppers leap

Fleas bounce
Spiders pounce

Worms wiggle
Gnats niggle

Bees bumble
Ladybirds rumble

Dragonflies flit
But I sit!

© Lynn Huggins-Cooper

©Corel

Further ideas
● Make minibeast hats to wear during your movement sessions. Cover balloons with paper mâché then cut them in half to make ladybird hats. Paint them red and add black dots, then seal with PVA glue. Add elastic to keep the hats in place. Alternatively, paint the hats black and add crêpe-paper spiders' legs!

Lynn Huggins-Cooper is a children's author and PGCE science/DT lecturer.

Creeping caterpillars

Have fun finding out about caterpillars and making your own hairy models with these creative ideas

Crazy caterpillars

Stepping Stone: work creatively on a large or small scale (CD).
Early Learning Goal: explore colour, texture, shape, form and space in two or three dimensions (CD).
Group size: four to six children.

What you need

Pictures of caterpillars; green tights (cut to stocking length) or stockings; compost; grass seed; elastic bands; poster paints; paintbrushes; blunted cocktail sticks or toothpicks; green grapes; cloves; leaves.

What to do

● Share the caterpillar pictures and explain that you are going make caterpillars using different materials.

● Demonstrate how to join several grapes together using the toothpicks, then add cloves for eyes. Invite the children to have a go themselves.
● Display the caterpillars on leaves.
● Invite the children to work as a group to make a large caterpillar. Encourage them to mix grass seeds and compost together in a tray. Ask individuals to stuff some of the mixture into the stocking. Tie the end securely, then let the children paint a face and patterns on their crazy caterpillar.
● Place the caterpillar in a tray near the window, water regularly and watch your caterpillar grow hair.

Support and extension

Hold the stocking open for younger children to stuff with compost and seeds. Let older children make caterpillar segments by securing elastic bands around the stuffed stocking.

Home links
● Provide the children with caterpillar outlines in a variety of sizes to take home. Encourage parents to help their children to decorate and cut out the caterpillars and find leaves of the correct size to accommodate each caterpillar. Glue the caterpillars on to the leaves.

© Rebecca Finn

Hunt the bug

Stepping Stone: develop a repertoire of actions by putting a sequence of movements together (CD).
Early Learning Goal: use their imagination in art and design, music, dance, imaginative and role play and stories (CD).
Group size: whole group.

What you need

A copy of *We're Going on A Bear Hunt* by Michael Rosen (Walker Books).

What to do

● Gather the children into a circle.
● Say a version of 'We're Going on a Bear Hunt', using the following words:

We're going on a minibeast hunt!
We're going to catch some big ones.
What a beautiful day!
Are you ready? OK!

Oh-oh! Grass!
Long, wavy grass.
We can't go over it.
We can't go under it.

Oh, no! We've got to go through it!
Swishy, swashy!
Swishy, swashy!
Swishy, swashy!

● Continue the rhyme, wading through a deep, cold river (splash, splosh!), struggling through thick, oozy mud (squelch, squerch!), finding your way through a big, dark forest (stumble, trip!), fighting through a swirling, whirling snowstorm (hoooo, woooo!) and entering a narrow, gloomy cave (tiptoe!).
● Encourage the children to make up some new actions for each verse.
● When you come to the last verse, where you say 'What's that?', invite older children to make up responses, for example, Green and hairy! Creeping about! It's a caterpillar! or Black and hairy! Crawling around! It's a spider!

Support and extension

Younger children may need to be shown actions at first. Encourage older children to suggest other areas that the hunt could take them to and make up appropriate actions.

Further ideas
● Visit *www.dltk-teach.com/books/hungrycaterpillar/felt_fun.htm* and print out the puppets to retell *The Very Hungry Caterpillar* by Eric Carle (Puffin Books).

● Create a minibeast garden using twigs, pebbles and leaves. Make playdough or Plasticine minibeasts and hide them in the 'garden'.

Kevin Kelman
is a deputy headteacher
and author.

Chapter 3
Growth

Young children love to watch things grow and change, and the ideas in this chapter provide the inspiration for much exploration and investigation about the growth of people, plants and animals.

I can use a pencil

I can use a pencil
and a knife and fork.

*(Mime drawing
and cutting and eating.)*

I can put my clothes on.
I can run and walk.

(Pretend to dress.)
(Run on the spot.)

I can fasten buttons up
I can brush my hair.

(Touch real or pretend buttons.)
(Pretend to brush hair.)

I can go to coffee shops
and use a proper chair.

(Look proud and sit smartly.)

I can talk to Granny
on the telephone.

(Use hand as telephone.)

I can butter bread myself,
all on my own.

(Pretend to spread.)
(Look proud.)

I can help around the house
and in the garden, too.

*(Mime sweeping
and digging.)*

I am happy growing up,
...how about you?

(Look pleased.)
(Point to each other.)

© Brenda Williams

New babies

Use these ideas to help the children think about the needs of babies and how they communicate those needs to others

I need a cuddle

Stepping Stone: express needs and feelings in appropriate ways (PSED).
Early Learning Goal: respond to significant experiences, showing a range of feelings when appropriate (PSED).
Group size: up to ten children.

What you need

Visiting parent and baby; pictures of babies; feeding bottle; nappies; blanket; cuddly toy.

What to do

● Invite a parent and baby into your setting.
● Encourage the children to discuss with the parent how the baby makes his needs felt. Does he cry in a different way if he needs feeding, compared to when he needs a nappy change? Does he kick his legs when he is cross? How does cuddling help the baby?
● Make a display of the pictures and baby equipment. Talk about the baby's needs as you position each item.
● Taking each need in turn, invite the children to say what they do or say when they are hungry, feel tired or cross, want a cuddle, have a pain or want to go to the toilet.

● Help the children to say how they feel and respond. Do they cry, become bad-tempered, throw a tantrum? Or do they ask for what they want?
● Explain that babies are asking when they cry, but older children can usually explain what they need.
● Discuss other times when they are unsure, shy or frightened, or just need a cuddle.

Support and extension

Use opportunities as they occur, encouraging younger children to talk about how they feel and what they need. Help older children to understand how others are feeling, too.

Home links
● Ask the children to bring in photographs of new family members for a display.

© Eyewire

Let's get dressed

Stepping Stone: demonstrate a sense of pride in own achievement (PSED).
Early Learning Goals: dress and undress independently and manage their own personal hygiene; select and use activities and resources independently (PSED).
Group size: up to five children.

What you need

Baby dolls; baby clothes for different seasons (night-time and daytime clothes); baby bath; warm, soapy water; towel.

What to do

● Talk about the things that an adult has to do for a baby, such as bathe them, feed them and clothe them. Why is it important to dress a baby in warm clothing if it is cold? What clothes would the baby

need to be dressed in if the weather was very hot? Why?
● Show the children the selection of clothes and discuss the different times of year when a baby might wear them.
● Ask each child to carefully bathe and dry a baby doll. Encourage the children to choose appropriate clothes for specific occasions, such as a cold winter's day or a hot summer's day.
● Talk about the sequence in which the clothes are put on, and the best ways of putting them on. Encourage the children to persevere with fastenings.

Support and extension

Remind younger children to sequence clothes when dressing themselves. Help older children to sort out clothes, such as jumpers, by placing them face down before putting them on.

Further ideas
● Invite the children to draw pictures of incidents when they have felt cross, sad or happy, and talk to the group about them.

● Make a display of things that we use to help keep babies clean, such as soap, talc, wipes and sponges.

Brenda Williams is an early years specialist and freelance writer.

Baby talk

From baby baths to board books, these activities will inspire the children to start talking about all sorts of baby accessories!

An early visitor

Stepping Stone: begin to use talk instead of action to rehearse, reorder and reflect on past experience, linking significant events from own experience and from stories, paying attention to sequence and how events lead into one another (CLL).

Early Learning Goal: use talk to organise, sequence and clarify thinking, ideas, feelings and events (CLL).

Group size: up to six children.

What you need

Visiting parent and baby; baby bath and accessories; paper; pen.

What to do

● Invite a parent to show the children how to bathe, change and dress a baby.

● Discuss the forthcoming visit and invite the children to recall their own experiences of babies.

● While the parent is bathing, changing and dressing their baby, consider the sequence of actions by asking the children to explain what is happening and what might happen next.

● After the visit, encourage the children to recall the event. Scribe their memories on to a sheet of paper.

● Consider any actions that have been omitted or written in the wrong order and encourage the children to fill in any gaps.

Support and extension

Invite younger children to watch a visiting baby playing with some toys, then talk about the choices that the baby made. Encourage older children to use appropriate vocabulary, such as 'first', 'next' and 'last', as they recall sequences of events.

© Dan Howell / Soda

Home links

● Ask parents to take their children to baby departments in shops to look at items for sale and draw their attention to labels and captions.

Babies' catalogues

Stepping Stone: hear and say the initial in words and know which letters represent some of the sounds (CLL).

Early Learning Goal: use their phonic knowledge to write simple regular words and make phonetically plausible attempts at more complex words (CLL).

Group size: four children.

What you need

Copy of *The Baby's Catalogue* by Janet Ahlberg (Puffin Books); mail order catalogues; toy catalogues; white paper; glue; glue spreaders; child scissors.

What to do

● Read *The Baby's Catalogue* to the children and talk about the things that a baby needs and enjoys.

● Suggest that the children make their own baby

catalogues by cutting or tearing pictures from toy and mail order catalogues. Encourage them to choose pictures based on their own experiences of babies' physical needs and the toys that they might play with.

● Ask the children to glue the pictures on to sheets of white paper, folded in half.

● When they are dry, join several sheets together to form little books.

● Invite the children to talk about the initial letter sounds of the items on the pages of their catalogues. Write the words for them, sounding out the letters as you do so.

Support and extension

Help younger children to cut out their pictures and let them make collages rather than a book. Encourage older children to write the initial letter sounds and attempt to write whole words beside the pictures in their babies' catalogues.

Further ideas

● Visit a baby clinic with the children.

● Invite a health visitor to come and talk about caring for babies.

Jean Evans
is an early years
consultant and author.

Rock-a-bye baby

Stepping Stone: listen to favourite nursery rhymes, stories and songs. Join in with repeated refrains, anticipating key events and important phrases (CLL).
Early Learning Goal: listen with enjoyment, and respond to stories, songs and other music, rhymes and poems and make up their own stories, songs, rhymes and poems (CLL).
Group size: up to ten children.

What you need
Just the children.

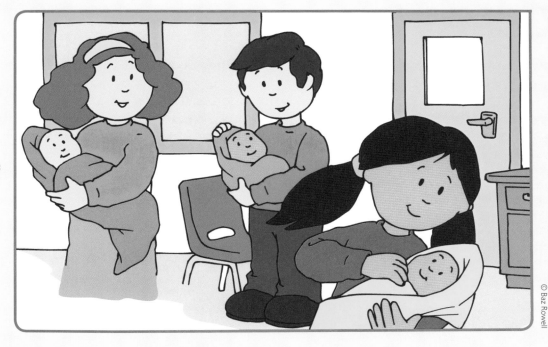

© Baz Rowell

What to do
● Explain how adults often sing lullabies to help their babies fall asleep.
● Sing the traditional rhyme 'Rock-a-bye Baby' with the children and invite them to pretend that they are rocking babies to sleep in their arms.
● Say the words of the rhyme slowly and ask whether the children think that the ending is happy. How do they think the baby will feel when the cradle falls out of the tree?

● Suggest that the children make up lullabies with happy endings. Start by adapting a well-known tune such as 'Here We Go Round the Mulberry Bush', changing the words to 'This is the way you go to sleep'.

Support and extension
Sing traditional baby action rhymes with younger children, such as 'This Little Piggy Went to Market', Round and Round the Garden Like a Teddy Bear' and 'Pat-a-cake, Pat-a-cake', encouraging them to join in with familiar words and actions. Make a book of 'Rhymes for babies' with older children and hang it in the home area to share with the dolls.

Baby books

Stepping Stone: show interest in illustrations and print in books and print in the environment (CLL).
Early Learning Goal: explore and experiment with sounds, words and texts (CLL).
Group size: four children.

What you need
Selection of books for babies, such as board books, cloth books, 'noisy' books and sponge bathtime books; water tray.

Preparation
Visit the library or bookshop to obtain an appropriate selection of books. Ask whether they can supply any free posters about books for babies. Display the books with the posters and signs indicating that they are for babies.

What to do
● Draw the children's attention to the words on the posters and captions. Tell them that these books are especially for babies.
● Look at the board books together. Explain that they are strong because they have to stand

constant handling and chewing by babies. Point out the pictures and words. Can the children suggest what the words say?
● Explore the other books on the table and find out how each type of book is different. For example, create sounds with 'noisy' books, lift flaps and try out bathtime books in the water tray.
● Notice and compare the different letters and words on the pages of each book.

Support and extension
Encourage younger children to choose a book to share with an adult, asking them to name the objects pictured and point to any letters that they can see. Suggest that older children 'read' the books to their younger friends.

Growth

Gone to seed

Find out about seeds, sorting, patterns, number and size with these fun maths activities

Fruity patterns

Stepping Stone: sustain interest for a length of time on a pre-decided construction or arrangement (MD).

Early Learning Goal: talk about, recognise and recreate simple patterns (MD).

Group size: four children.

© Photodisc, Inc.

What you need
Selection of fruits with small seeds, such as watermelon, pomegranate and pumpkin; paper; glue; children's cutlery; sharp knife (adult use).

What to do
● Cut the fruit into quarters. Talk about the different seeds that you find, noticing their shape and the patterns that they make inside the fruit.
● Help the children to collect the seeds from the fruit using the small cutlery.
● Let the children create patterns with the seeds. Challenge them to copy the patterns in the fruit. Can they make circles, ovals and spirals of seeds? Encourage them to give the seeds in place on to the paper.
● Make some patterns using alternating seeds, for example, first a pumpkin seed then a pomegranate pip and so on.

Support and extension
Draw an outline on the paper for the younger children to fill with seeds. Talk with older children about other fruits and their seeds. Where are the seeds on a strawberry or in a banana?

Home links
● Send home a few radish seeds for each child to grow. They can be grown in an old plastic carton or in the garden. Encourage the children to bring their crop to your setting.

● Write out the finger rhyme, 'Five Little Peas in a Pea-pod Pressed' from *This Little Puffin...* compiled by Elizabeth Matterson (Puffin Books) for the parents' noticeboard. Encourage them to say the rhyme at home with their children.

Further ideas
● Collect some seed catalogues and old gardening magazines. Cut out pictures of seed packets and sort into fruit and vegetables, or perhaps by colour.

● Use a growbag and a packet of mixed annual seeds, and create your own mini garden from seed.

Pop those peas

Stepping Stone: say with confidence the number that is one more than a given number (MD).

Early Learning Goal: in practical activities and discussion, begin to use the vocabulary involved in adding and subtracting (MD).

Group size: four children.

What you need
Simple outlines of four baby bird shapes with features drawn on; scissors; peapods for shelling; four small dishes; *Meg's Veg* by Helen Nicoll and Jan Pienkowski (Puffin Books).

What to do
● Cut out the four baby bird shapes and place them in the centre of the table.
● Read *Meg's Veg* to the children. Discuss what Meg's seeds needed to grow.

● Give each child a bowl and a peapod to shell. Invite them, in turn, to count the number of peas inside their pod and give just those peas to one of the baby birds.
● When everyone has placed their peas on a baby bird, shell more peas and let each child fill their bowl.
● Count the number of peas that each bird has and talk about how many the birds will have if you give them one more. Give the birds one more and count again.
● Talk about which bird has the most peas, which has lots of peas and which has a few.

Support and extension
Help younger children to give each baby bird three peas, counting with them as they place each pea on to the shape. Ask older children to place the birds in order from which has the most peas to which has the least.

Clare Beswick
is an early years and childcare consultant.

Cress numbers

Stepping Stone: recognise numerals 1 to 5, then 1 to 9 (MD).
Early Learning Goal: recognise numerals 1 to 9 (MD).
Group size: five children.

What you need

Blotting paper or kitchen roll; kitchen foil; ten pieces of card (approximately 10cm x 10cm); tiny jug; cress seeds; dark paper; pen; children's scissors.

What to do

● Cover each piece of card on one side with foil. Fold any remaining foil underneath the card.
● Draw a large numeral from 1 to 10 on each piece of blotting paper. If you do not have blotting paper use a double thickness of kitchen roll.
● Help the children to cut out two numerals each.

● Place each numeral on to a sheet of foil-covered card. Let the children dampen each numeral with a little water and sprinkle cress seeds on top.
● Cover the seed numerals over with dark paper and check each day. Keep the blotting paper damp and in a day or two the seeds will start to sprout. At this point, remove the dark paper and place in a sunny place.
● Talk about the numerals as the children work. Encourage them to count objects and people that they see, for example, how many children are painting, and then find the matching numeral.

Support and extension

Help younger children with the cutting by holding the numeral with them as they cut. Ask older children to find other matching numerals from around your setting, perhaps in books, on signs or on the telephone.

Off the allotment

Stepping Stone: order two items by weight or capacity (MD).
Early Learning Goal: use language such as 'greater', 'smaller', 'heavier' or 'lighter' to compare quantities (MD).
Group size: four children.

What you need

Selection of fruit and vegetables such as melon, apple, grapes, runner beans and avocado; children's cutlery; play-dough tools; small sieve; dishes; sharp knife (adult use).

What to do

● Cut the melon into segments, each with some seeds.
● Let the children explore all the fruit and vegetables freely, using the cutlery and dough tools to collect the seeds.
● Talk to them about the different shapes and sizes of the seeds. Which fruit and vegetables do the children like? Where are the seeds in the favourite fruit and vegetables? Which fruit has the most seeds?
● Can they free the avocado stone? Feel the weight of the different seeds. Which is the heaviest? Can they find the lightest?

Support and extension

Help younger children to use the cutlery and tools safely. Count the seeds together. Encourage older children to think about which fruit has the most seeds and which has the heaviest seeds.

Growth

Blooming marvellous!

Play at nature detectives and investigate signs of new growth using these activity ideas

Out and about

Stepping Stone: show an interest in the world in which they live (KUW).
Early Learning Goal: find out about their environment, and talk about those features they like and dislike (KUW).
Group size: variable, but at least one adult for every two children.

What you need
Adult helpers; camera; books and pictures about spring; local area where you can enjoy a safe walk.

What to do
● Look at the books and pictures about spring. Introduce the children to the names of spring flowers and talk about the signs of new life.
● Explain that you are going on a walk to look for signs of new life after the long winter. Emphasise safety rules before leaving.
● Enjoy your walk together, noticing buds bursting on trees, spring flowers in gardens and weeds pushing through cracks in pavements.
● Take photographs of the children's discoveries during the walk.
● Back at your setting, recall what you saw. Over the following days, encourage the children to paint and draw what they can remember from their walk.

● Develop the photographs and display them on a low board so that the children can discuss them together.

Support and extension
Shorten the walk for younger children. Encourage older children to take the photographs themselves or to carry clipboards so that they can make observational drawings during the walk.

© 2004/Solveig Stibbe/Alamy.com Angela Maynard

Home links
● Suggest that parents point out new growth in the ground and on trees in gardens and parks.

St David's Day

Stepping Stone: gain an awareness of the cultures and beliefs of others (KUW).
Early Learning Goal: begin to know about their own cultures and beliefs and those of other people (KUW).
Group size: up to six children.

What you need
Daffodils growing in a bowl; small trowel; leeks with roots intact; resources relating to Welsh culture, such as a Welsh doll and flag.

What to do
● Set up a table display about the Welsh culture and share the items with the children.
● Explain how Welsh people enjoy songs and music, and wear the national symbol of either a daffodil or leek on St David's Day (1 March 2004).

● Show the children the bowl of daffodils,
● Explain that spring is a time when seeds and bulbs begin to shoot as the soil gets warmer.
● Lift a daffodil out gently with a trowel and shake off any loose soil. Let the children look closely at the roots, bulb, shoot, leaves and flower. (Be careful not to touch the bulb as it is poisonous.)
● Invite the children to help you to gently put it back into the soil and firm it into place.
● Now look closely at a leek. Smell it and talk about the long string-like roots. How is it similar to the daffodil? How is it different?

Support and extension
Focus on sensory comparisons between a daffodil and leek with younger children. Let older children draw the daffodil and label the different parts.

Further ideas
● Make leek and potato soup.

● Hold an Eisteddfod (a traditional Welsh festival of music and poetry) and enjoy dancing and singing.

Jean Evans
is an early years consultant and author.

Flights of fancy

Develop small and large motor skills as you enjoy these activities based on the colour and movement of butterflies

Flutterbies

Stepping Stone: move freely with pleasure and confidence (PD).
Early Learning Goal: move with confidence, imagination and in safety (PD).
Group size: whole group.

What you need
Book, poster or video about the life cycle of a butterfly, such as *The Crunching, Munching Caterpillar* by Sheridan Cain and Jack Tickle (Little Tiger Press); music to inspire a butterfly dance such as 'Sleepers Awake' (Cantata 140 – Bach) or 'Largo Al Factotum' (Barber of Seville – Rossini) both from a CD called Classic Commercials (available from www.amazon.co.uk; tape or CD player; brightly-coloured scarves, ribbons or crêpe paper.

What to do
● Using your chosen book, poster or video, look at and discuss the life cycle of a butterfly with the children.
● In an open space, invite the children to mime the different stages: being an egg (curled up tight in a little ball), then a caterpillar (crawling to find food, getting sleepy, spinning a cocoon), and finally a butterfly (excited, full of energy, fluttering around in the sunshine, drinking nectar from flowers).
● Play a piece of music and invite the children to use dance to show the different stages of the butterfly's life.
● When everyone has had a turn, let all the children hold scarves, ribbons or crêpe-paper strips and enjoy pretending to be butterflies, fluttering around excitedly and visiting imaginary flowers!

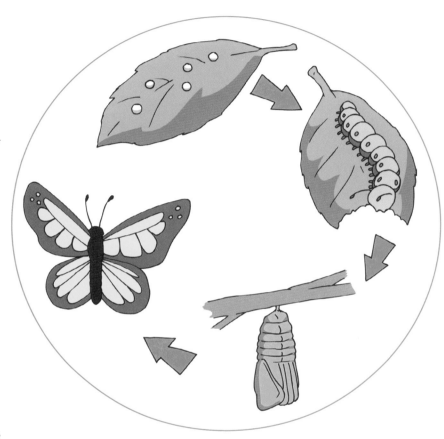

Support and extension
Encourage younger children to watch the rest of the group before joining in the dance. Invite older children to perform their dance sequence to the rest of the group.

Is that a butterfly?
Stepping Stone: engage in activities requiring hand–eye co-ordination (PD).
Early Learning Goal: handle tools, objects, construction and malleable materials safely and with increasing control (PD).
Group size: whole group.

What you need
Lollipop sticks; sticky tape; butterfly stencils; paper; scissors; colouring materials; brown wool or paint; cardboard tubes cut to just over half the length of a lollipop stick; story about butterflies, such as *The Very Hungry Caterpillar* by Eric Carle (Puffin Books).

What to do
● Read your chosen story to the children. Invite them to share their experiences of butterflies.
● Give each child a piece of paper and a pencil, then encourage them to draw around a butterfly stencil on their paper. Invite them to colour it in with a symmetrical pattern.
● Help each child to carefully cut out their butterfly then tape it to a lollipop stick.
● Using brown paint, or glue and brown wool, ask each child to decorate a cardboard tube to look like a pupa.
● Invite the children to gently fold the wings of their butterfly. Slide the pupae over the butterflies and enjoy 'hatching' them by popping them out of their cocoons!

Support and extension
Give younger children hands-on help where necessary. Let older children use a selection of collage materials to make their cocoons more realistic.

Home links
● Give parents instructions for making grassy caterpillars with their children. Plant grass seed into five plastic cups filled with soil. Decorate one cup as the head of a caterpillar, then water and watch them grow into a hairy caterpillar's body!

Further ideas
● Explore other animal life cycles such as frogs, spiders and silkworms using posters, videos and books.

Martine Horvath is a Reception teacher and early years educational consultant.

Growth
All of a twitter

Focus on textures and sounds with these hands-on activities all about baby birds

Nest builders

Stepping Stone: experiment to create different textures (CD).

Early Learning Goal: explore colour, texture, shape, form and space in two and three dimensions (CD).

Group size: four children.

What you need

Natural materials such as twigs, feathers, moss and leaves; plastic garden netting; string; card; paint; paintbrushes; collage materials; play dough; scissors; glue.

What to do

● Talk about birds' nests with the children. Why do birds build nests? How do they make them?

● Tell the children that they are going to use different materials to make their own nests.

● Help them to cut circles of garden netting, approximately 25cm in diameter. Pull the sides of the netting up to make a nest shape, and secure with lengths of string.

© Photodisc. inc

● Encourage the children to weave the different natural materials through the netting. Talk about the different textures and effects that the children achieve.

● Let the children make eggs and chicks for their nests from the card, collage materials or play dough.

● Encourage the children to experiment with different effects, such as dripping paint on to card egg-shapes, or adding collage materials to a play-dough chick for a feather effect.

● Display your nests and eggs on a table and let the children add to them as they find other textured materials.

Support and extension

Play alongside younger children and help them to manipulate the materials to achieve their aims. Encourage older children to collect additional materials from their garden or around your setting.

Home links
● Invite parents to help their children to collect materials suitable for the nest-building activity.

● Ask parents to listen for and talk about bird-song when they are out and about with their children.

Two little dicky birds

Stepping Stone: sing to themselves and make up simple songs (CD).

Early Learning Goal: recognise and explore how sounds can be changed, sing simple songs from memory, recognise repeated sounds and sound patterns and match movements to music (CD).

Group size: up to eight children.

What you need

Two large sheets of tissue paper; four metal spoons; two shakers.

Preparation

Familiarise yourself with the traditional rhyme 'Two Little Dicky Birds'.

What to do

● Sing the rhyme with the children using the traditional finger actions.

● Ask the children how they could use the paper to make a 'fly away' sound, for example, waft it, blow on it or scrunch it up.

● Say the rhyme again together, this time inviting two children to add the 'fly away' sounds at the appropriate points.

● Experiment with the spoons and the shakers.

● Ask the children how the baby birds might be feeling, for example, hungry, tired or excited.

● Change the rhyme to fit the children's ideas, for example, 'Two baby birds sitting in the nest, one all excited and the other one sleepy, fly away Peter, sleep tight Paul, come back Peter, wake up Paul'.

Support and extension

Vary the rhyme by using younger children's own names, and encourage them to imitate the actions. Let older children add the names of different types of birds to the rhyme, such as robin and wren, instead of Peter and Paul.

Further ideas
● Look at pictures of different eggs, and try to recreate the colours and patterns using sponge and bubble painting.

Clare Beswick is an early years and childcare consultant.

Chapter 4
Weather

Make the most of our ever changing climate with these fun weather activities. There are language ideas for rainy days, maths activities based on sunny weather and some lively movement ideas that capture the excitement of thunder and lightning!

Rain means puddles!

Rain means puddles!   *(Imitate rain with fingers.)*
Puddles mean fun.
Splashing in my wellies   *(Mime splashing, jumping and running around.)*
As I jump and run.

Snow means snowballs!   *(Mime picking up snow and moulding into a ball.)*
Snowballs to throw.   *(Pretend to throw.)*
Throw them at the snowman   *(Stand stiffly, smiling, like a snowman.)*
In the deep crisp snow.

Wind means flying!   *(Make swirling movements with arms.)*
Flying my kite.
Bucking and blowing   *(Pretend to hold on to kite and look upwards.)*
As I hold on tight.

Sun means picnics!   *(Pretend to eat.)*
Barbecues and buns.
Paddling at the seaside   *(Mime lifting skirt or trousers to paddle.)*
Races to be run.   *(Run on the spot.)*

© Brenda Williams

Clothes for all weathers

Enjoy some dressing-up fun as the children dress themselves independently for different weather conditions

What are you wearing?

Stepping Stone: take initiatives and manage developmentally appropriate tasks (PSED).
Early Learning Goal: dress and undress independently (PSED).
Group size: six to eight children.

What you need

Rucksack; carrier bags; variety of children's clothing and footwear, such as sandals, wellies, scarf, gloves, hat, cardigan, socks and jacket.

What to do

● Wrap each clothing item, or pair of items, in an individual carrier bag, then place in the rucksack.
● Ask the children to remove their socks and footwear.
● Gather in a circle. Explain that you have been shopping and you have placed all your purchases in the rucksack. Pass the rucksack around the circle inviting each child to select and remove a carrier bag and open it up.
● Ask the children to name the item of clothing inside the carrier bag and place it on the appropriate part of their body.
● Continue around the circle until all the items have been used up. Encourage the children to cheer when their peers put the item on the correct part of their body.
● Ask the children to take off the items of clothing and replace them back in the carrier bags and then into the rucksack. Play the game again so that everyone has the chance to try on different items of clothing.

© Derek Cooknell

Home links

● Ask carers to supply photographs from family holidays. Talk about different weather conditions and clothes that were worn.

Support and extension

Support younger children when they are putting the clothes and footwear on. Older and more able children will be able to take off and put on their outdoor clothing themselves when arriving and leaving your setting. Encourage this by providing a personal peg or coat hanger.

Further ideas

● Find information books with pictures of people from different climates, such as desert or polar regions, and look at the clothes they wear.

● Encourage the children to dress and undress the dolls in your setting, naming each item of clothing.

What shall I wear?

Stepping Stone: show care and concern for self (PSED).
Early Learning Goal: have a developing awareness of their own needs (PSED).
Group size: six to eight children.

What you need

Information books about weather; wellies; shorts; woolly hat; waterproof coat; a simple A4 drawing of a child wearing just underwear (make a copy for each child); old catalogues from children's clothing outlets; glue; scissors.

What to do

● Gather the group together on the floor and look at the books and poster. Discuss the different types of weather conditions that we experience in our climate.

● Show the children the wellies, shorts, woolly hat and waterproof coat. On what kind of day would they wear each item?
● Invite the children to talk about the other clothes they wear on a hot day, a wet day, a snowy day and so on.
● Explain that you want each child to choose a type of weather and to find pictures of suitable clothing. Give each child a copy of the photocopied sheet. Encourage them to look through the catalogues to find appropriate clothes to cut out and stick on the body shape.

Support and extension

Support younger children by providing pre-cut clothing pictures. Children who are more confident with emergent writing can write a story to go with the picture describing the weather conditions.

Kevin Kelman
is a deputy headteacher and writer.

Rainy day adventures!

Delight in the sounds and sensations of a rainy day with these exciting language and literacy activities

Rainy day rhymes

Stepping Stone: listen to favourite nursery rhymes, stories and songs (CLL).

Early Learning Goal: listen with enjoyment and respond to rhymes (CLL).

Group size: up to four children.

What you need

A rainy day; large sheet of paper cut into an umbrella shape; felt-tipped pens; crayons; poems or rhymes about rain, for example: 'Incy Wincy Spider'.

What to do

● Share some rainy day poems. Talk about the words used and how they make us think of the sounds of a rainy day.

● Take the children outside to listen to the rain. What can they hear? How do they feel? What can they see? They might suggest people swishing through puddles, water dripping, stamping and sloshing. Record the children's words and phrases.

● Back inside, gather around the table and work with the children to arrange their words and phrases into a poem. Keep it simple, use lots of repetition and include as many of the children's words as possible. For example:

Pitter, patter, splish, splosh
Wellie boots and macintosh
Rain goes drip drip
Tyres go swish swish
Wellies go stamp, stamp,
We love a rainy day.

© Gaynor Berry

● Once you are happy with your poem, write it out clearly in large letters on the umbrella shaped paper. Let the children decorate it with patterns and pictures.

● Display on the wall for everyone to enjoy.

Support and extension

Let younger children enjoy the moment and help them to describe their emotions at the time. Help older children to record their words and feelings on their own pieces of umbrella-shaped paper.

Further ideas

● Put a shallow water tray out during a downpour and watch it fill up together. Talk about the sounds that you hear and use language to describe the water as it fills the container from empty to full and overflowing.

● Collect some rainwater and use it to water plants and seedlings in your setting.

Home links

● Ask carers to help their children to collect rainwater in a plastic bottle. Let the children add their rainwater to a tall cylinder and use in your rainy day display.

Whatever the weather

Stepping Stone: use language for an increasing range of purposes (CLL).

Early Learning Goal: speak clearly and audibly with confidence and control (CLL).

Group size: up to six children.

What you need

Large box or basket with clothes for all weathers, such as wellies, sun hat, scarf, shorts, thick coat, waterproof mac, swimsuit, mittens and sunglasses; cards illustrated by the children to represent sun, snow or rain; a large mirror.

What to do

● Let the children take turns to pick a card and then select and put on an item of clothing that is appropriate for that weather. Go around the group, encouraging the children to describe what they need to choose from the box and why.

● When the box is empty, invite the children, in turn, to look in the mirror and describe what they are wearing.

● Ask the children to return clothes by category. For example: 'Let's put all the sun clothes back.'

● Share the hilarity of the game as the children become entangled in some very mixed-up outfits!

● Make the game available to the children after the session. Observe how they use the resources and organize and monitor their own turn-taking.

Support and extension

Younger children love to find matching pairs, such as two sandals or gloves from a box of objects. Older children could follow a sequence of objects on cards and dress themselves from the box accordingly.

Trickles and trails

Stepping Stone: question why things happen and give explanations (CLL).
Early Learning Goal: respond to what they have seen and heard by relevant comments or questions (CLL).
Group size: up to eight children.

What you need

A rainy day; lengths of string; strips of Cellophane; large brushes; bucket of assorted small cars and other rollers.

What to do

● On a rainy day, dress appropriately and go outside. Watch the rain trickling down window panes, stamp in puddles and make footprints.
● Talk about the patterns that the rain is making. Why does the water trickle down the window? What happens when two raindrops join together? Can the children change the path of the water?
● Help the children to use the resources to make patterns and shapes with the puddles and rainwater. Roll the cars or drag lengths of string through the puddles. What happens? Help the children to develop their own ideas about why the trails get fainter and maybe disappear.
● Encourage each child to describe their patterns and how they created them.

© Comstock

Support and extension

The youngest children will delight in following wet footprints, while older children can compare and describe the different footprints. Use language of comparative size and help the children to identify the different patterns and matching pairs.

Splish, splash, splosh

Stepping Stone: build up vocabulary that reflects the breadth of their experiences (CLL).
Early Learning Goal: extend their vocabulary, exploring the meanings and sounds of new words (CLL).
Group size: four children.

What you need

Shallow tray of water or individual trays; play people and accessories; small sieves and colanders; plastic tea strainers; watering cans; small plastic spoons; small Lego houses; toy cars.

What to do

● Carefully arrange the water play to represent wet weather street scenes.
● Play alongside the children. Add a commentary for a few minutes, describing the children's activity and encouraging them to join in.
● Introduce new words to describe what you are seeing and hearing.
● Encourage the children to compare the sounds of, for example, 'rain' from the watering can or play people splashing through 'puddles'. Can they make a sound like the rain trickling from the sieve, or plopping on to the rooftops of the houses?

Support and extension

Encourage younger children to develop simple symbolic play by modelling simple actions and then encouraging imitation. Help older children to record their activity in words and pictures on a large shared sheet of paper.

© Gaynor Berry

Clare Beswick is an early years consultant.

Bring me sunshine!

Develop a range of mathematical skills with this selection of fun activities for sunny days

Picnic time

Stepping Stone: listen to favourite nursery rhymes, stories and songs (MD).
Early Learning Goal: use language such as 'circle' or 'bigger' to describe the shape and size of solid and flat shapes (MD).
Group size: four to six children.

What you need

Bread; soft spread; fillings such as jam or cheese spread (NB check for allergies and dietary requirements); blunt knives; plates.

Preparation

Wash all equipment and surfaces are and ask the children to wash their hands thoroughly.

What to do

● Explain that you are going to make some sandwiches for a picnic (indoors or out).
● As the children spread the bread, talk about its shape and properties. How many corners does it have? Does all bread have corners?
● Once the spreading is complete invite the children to add their choice of filling and sandwich the bread together.
● Remind the children what shape the bread is. Can they cut it into smaller sandwiches that are a different shape? Encourage them to plan ahead and discuss the shape that they want to produce.
● Talk about the end results before putting the food on plates and enjoying your own picnic to close the session.

© Derek Cooknell

Support and extension

Model mathematical language yourself to encourage very young children to use it. Invent challenges for older children by asking them to make six square sandwiches, two triangles and two rectangles or eight triangles.

Home links

● Add suitable times such as 8 o'clock and 5 o'clock to the weather chart, and let children take a copy home to complete with their carers. Bring the charts back after a week to share with the group.

Sunshine or clouds?

Stepping Stone: count actions or objects that cannot be moved (MD).
Early Learning Goal: count reliably up to ten everyday objects (MD).
Group size: two children.

What you need

A dice; 20 cards (approximately 8cm square) with a sun on one side and a cloud on the other.

What to do

● Show the cards to the children and talk about the pictures. Explain that you are going to play a game. Let the children choose whether to be a 'sun' or a 'cloud'.
● Spread out the cards on the table so that there are ten cards showing clouds and ten showing suns.
● Ask the first child to roll the dice and count the spots. Let the child turn over the appropriate number of cards to change the pictures. For example, if she has chosen to be the sun, she turns over cloud cards to make more suns. She then passes the dice to the other child.
● Continue playing until all the cards show the same picture and a winner is declared.
● Alternatively, set a time limit and then count the suns and clouds to find a winner.

Support and extension

Use a dice with just 1, 2 or 3 spots for younger children and just ten cards in total. Use a number dice for more able children. Periodically check who is ahead and by how many.

Further ideas

● Use play dough to make different shaped cakes and biscuits for a pretend picnic.

● Set up an ice-cream stall and use real pennies for buying and selling.

What is it like today?

Stepping Stone: use their own methods to solve a problem (MD).
Early Learning Goal: use language such as 'more' or 'less' to compare two amounts (MD).
Group size: whole group.

What you need
A blank weather chart (see 'preparation'); clock; drawing materials.

Preparation
Draw a simple weather chart with five rows (one for each day) and two columns (morning and afternoon). Draw symbols to represent 'sunny', 'rainy' and 'windy' above the chart. Label each symbol.

© Soda/David Franck

What to do
● Look at the empty chart with the children. Discuss what it is for and how to use it.
● Decide on a time in the morning and afternoon when you will check the weather. Explain that you must all keep an eye on the clock and remind each other when it is time to check the weather.
● Each day at the allotted time, look at the weather together and choose a child to decide upon an appropriate symbol and draw it in the correct space.

● At the end of the week, discuss the completed chart. Count the different symbols and discuss how many more or less there are of each kind.
● Encourage the children to pose questions of their own using the words 'more' and 'less'.

Support and extension
Ask younger children specific questions, for example: 'Are there more suns or more clouds?'. Extend older or more able children's vocabulary by including 'most' and 'least'.

Lollipop games

Stepping Stone: say with confidence the number that is one more than a given number (MD).
Early Learning Goal: begin to use the vocabulary involved in adding and subtracting (MD).
Group size: six to eight children.

What you need
At least ten cardboard ice lolly outlines in different shapes and colours; Blu-Tack.

What to do
● Count the lollies and talk about their shapes and colours. Give each child a lolly and keep the rest yourself. Play 'show me' games, asking the children to hold up their lolly if it is a certain shape or colour.
● Blu-Tack your lollies to the wall and count them together. Ask a 'show me' question and count how many of the children's lollies fit the criteria. How many lollies will there be altogether if you add the 'show me' lollies to the wall?
● Invite the children to stick the extra lollies on the wall and check the total by counting. Continue until all the lollies are on the wall.

● Finish by removing the lollies from the wall as you sing: 'Ten ice lollies standing in the sun (repeat). If one ice lolly should start to melt and run, there'd be nine ice lollies standing in the sun'.

Support and extension
Work with smaller groups of young children, using fewer lollies. Challenge more able children with more complex problem-solving questions such as, 'If I put three more lollies on the wall but one fell off, how many would there be?'.

© Gaynor Berry

Barbara J Leach
is former head of a
4+ Unit in Leicestershire.

Weather

Frosty fun

Make the most of the cold weather with these investigations into snow and ice!

Sensing snow

Stepping Stone: examine objects and living things to find out more about them (KUW).

Early Learning Goal: investigate objects and materials using all of their senses as appropriate (KUW).

Group size: four to six children.

What you need

Clipboards; dark fabric; magnifying glasses; storage box; a snowy day!

What to do

● On snowy days, take the opportunity to gather snow in cartons and store it in the freezer.

● If you have a snowy or very frosty day, suggest that the children go out to explore. Dress warmly, and give each child a clipboard covered in dark fabric and a magnifying glass.

● Ideally, go out when snow is falling and catch some flakes on the clipboard. Otherwise show the children how to pick up a few snowflakes gently to put on to the clipboard.

● Examine them under the magnifying glass. What do they look like? Can you see any patterns?

● Put the clipboards and magnifying glasses in the storage box and ask the children to walk over the snow. Does it make a noise as they walk to it? Pick up some snow and smell it. Discover how it feels on warm hands and falling softly on to faces. Warn against tasting the snow.

© Comstock

Support and extension

Younger children will explore snow properties themselves as they play outdoors on a snowy day. Ask appropriate questions related to their sensory experiences as they do so. Encourage older children to record their observations through drawing pictures and help them by scribing their words for them.

Frozen or melted?

Stepping Stone: talk about what is seen and what is happening (KUW).

Early Learning Goal: ask questions about why things happen and how things work (KUW).

Group size: four to six children.

What you need

Ice cubes; insulating materials including tissue, foil, bubble wrap, small towel and Thermos flask; fridge with freezer compartment; small bowls.

What to do

● Show the children a bowl of ice cubes. What do they look like? Leave the bowl for a short time then look again. What has happened? Introduce the word 'melting'. Does anyone know what this means? How could you stop the ice cubes melting?

● Sit around the table with the bowls and insulating materials in the centre. Put some cubes into four individual bowls and wrap the rest in the materials. Put one bowl outside, one on a sunny windowsill, one in the fridge and another in the freezer compartment. Can the children predict what will happen to each group of ice cubes?

● Return to the activity regularly during the session and discuss what is happening. Which cubes are still frozen? Have any melted completely? Why? Introduce the word 'insulate' and explain the meaning. Which object or material was the most successful insulator? How can you tell?

Support and extension

Give younger children just two options such as a flask and a bowl on a sunny windowsill. Talk to older children about how insulation can also keep things warm and discuss how they could insulate themselves against the cold weather in winter.

Home links

● Ask carers to let children help to make ice lollies or ice cubes at home.

Further ideas

● Freeze plastic animals in ice and watch them melt in the water tray.

● Blow bubbles outdoors on a very cold day and watch ice crystals form on them.

Jean Evans is an early years consultant and author.

Thunder and lightning

Focus on the movement and energy of the weather with these activities to develop fine and gross motor skills

Rain dance

Stepping Stone: respond to rhythm, music and story by means of gesture and movement (PD).

Early Learning Goal: move with confidence, imagination and in safety (PD).

Group size: whole group.

What you need

Large space (indoor or outdoor with appropriate clothing); drum and beater; tambourine or shaker; pictures of lightning and storms.

What to do

● Show the children the pictures of lightning and draw attention to the zigzag shapes. Challenge them to move their arms to make their own zigzag shapes.

● Explain that lightning moves quickly from the clouds to the ground. Ask the children to stretch up high and make fast zigzag movements going down to the ground. Invite a few children to demonstrate and then repeat the movements.

● Tell the children that lightning can cover huge areas before it strikes. Encourage them to run in zigzag lines, without touching anyone else, stopping sharply when you beat the drum. Practise the movements several times.

● Next, explain that when you shake the tambourine the children should move like lightning, and when they hear the drum they should stretch up tall and zigzag down to the ground. Repeat several times, selecting different children to demonstrate and to play the instruments.

© Gaynor Berry

● Conclude by sitting quietly, and maybe listening to some 'thunder storm' music!

Support and extension

Keep groups small for younger children and demonstrate zigzag movements for them. Older children could move in pairs, holding hands.

Home links

● Ask carers to send in leftover wool and threads for the sewing activity.

Stitching up the weather!

Stepping Stone: use one-handed tools and equipement (PD).

Early Learning Goal: handle tools and objects with increasing control (PD).

Group size: three children.

What you need

Sheets of paper; a bradawl or large needle (adult use); large blunt needles; selection of bright threads; scissors.

What to do

● Give each child a piece of card and encourage them to draw a rainy day picyure in the bottom quarter of the card. Explain to the children that they are going to sew lines on their picture to look like rain.

● Draw five or six vertical lines from the top of each card down to the picture to represent rain.

● An adult should punch several holes in each line, approximately 2 cm apart.

● Look at the different threads and talk about colours and thicknesses. Which colours and thicknesses could you use to represent the rain? Give out the blunt needles and stress safety issues aspects of keeping them low and away from eyes.

● Demonstrate how to thread a needle and knot the thread. On a demonstration card, show the children how to sew up through one hole and down through the next to form the stitches.

● Let each child choose and cut a length of thread and talk about where they will sew it. Help them to thread their needles. Start each child off and help them with the first stitches, then supervise as they sew their own pictures.

Support and extension

Let younger children choose their colours. Help them to cut the lengths, then thread the needles and knot the ends for them. Let older children draw in extra details such as a sun or rainbow, to their cards. Make the holes for them then let them stitch their own designs.

Further ideas

● Let the children add calendar booklets to their sewn pictures and take home to give as gifts.

Pauline Kenyon is an education consultant and writer.

It's a breeze!

Young children love to see the effects of the wind, so harness their enthusiasm by making objects that move and twirl in the breeze

Colourful twirlers

Stepping Stone: make constructions, collages, paintings, drawings and dances (CD)
Early Learning Goal: explore colour, texture, shape, form and space in two or three dimensions (CD).
Group size: four to six children.

What you need
Card (approximately 15cm by 8cm); strips of crêpe paper, paper tissue, ribbon or foil (approximately 1cm wide and of varying lengths); glue; scissors; single-hole hole-punch; thread.

Preparation
● Make a twirler by pasting strips of coloured materials on to the card. Do this on both sides. Cut about halfway up the centre of the card and punch a hole in the top. Fold one half of the card forwards and one back and add thread (see diagram).

What to do
● On a windy day, go outside and watch the effect of the wind. What happens to the branches of the trees? Notice how the wind picks up small leaves or other light items and spins them around.
● Back inside, demonstrate your twirler. Invite the

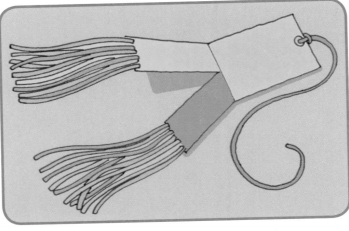

children to make their own colourful spinners.
● Invite the children to choose the materials to glue on to their card. Once the glue is dry, help them to cut up the centre of their pieces of card and punch a hole at the top.
● Show the children how to make the folds or encourage them to look at your model to see how to do it themselves then go outside and twirl!

Support and extension
Use glue sticks with younger children to cut down the drying time. Encourage older children to think carefully about the materials that they choose, perhaps arranging the strips in a pattern.

Fish kite

Stepping Stone: work creatively on a small scale (CD).
Early Learning Goal: explore colour, texure, shape, form and space in two or three dimensions (CD).
Group size: four children.

What you need
Tissue paper in various colours; florists' wire; glue; scissors; sticky tape; thread; felt-tipped pens.

Preparation
Cut large ovals of the same size (two per child), scales, fins and tails from the tissue paper.

What to do
● Begin by talking about kites. Does anyone have a kite at home? If possible, let the children experience flying a kite.
● Invite the children to make their own fish kites. Let each child choose a pair of tissue ovals and show them how to glue them together around the edges.
● Cut off a small tail section and a larger mouth section to allow a good flow of air through the fishes' bodies.
● Invite the children to select scales to glue on to both sides of their fish, fins, a tail and an eye on each side.
● Finally, an adult should line the fishes' lips with florists' wire, secure with sticky tape, and form it into a gaping mouth.
● Attach thread and then enjoy flying the fish outside on a windy day.

Support and extension
Remind young children that tissue paper is delicate and requires gentle application of tiny amounts of glue. Encourage older children to sketch their fish design before they begin.

Home links
● Ask whether anyone can lend the group a wind chime. Set up an area where the children can quietly listen to the gentle sounds made by the chime in a breeze.

Further idea
● Tape paper securely to an easel. Use runny paint outdoors on a windy day and watch the effect.

Barbara J Leach is former head of a 4+ Unit in Leicestershire.

© Gaynor Berry

Chapter 5
Festivals

The activities in this chapter will help you to bring a range of multicultural festivals right into your setting, enabling the children to experience the sights, sounds and traditions associated with a variety of colourful celebrations.

Janamashtami

Tonight is Janamashtami! *(Stand, looking patient.)*
But for now I have to wait
Tonight is Janamashtami
And I shall stay up late! *(Join hands in a circle and dance around.)*

We shall decorate the mandir
With flowers and with lights *(Stand still. Move hands in wide circles.)*
But for now I'm so excited
I am dancing in delight! *(Join hands in a circle and dance around.)*

Baby Krishna's in his cradle
And still hidden, out of sight *(Stand still. Place fingers on lips.)*
But I shall be so happy
When we look at him tonight! *(Join hands in a circle and dance around.)*

Tonight is Janamashtami!
And I'm jumping now with joy! *(Jump around.)*
For tonight I'll rock the cradle
Of this special baby boy. *(Join hands in a circle and dance around.)*

© Brenda Williams

© Jenny Tulip

Janamashtami (observed August-September) is a Hindu celebration of the birthday of Krishna, symbol of love who fights against evil. He can be a mischievous god who plays tricks on friends. A small cradle is covered with a cloth that is removed at midnight. Everyone rocks the cradle and leaves gifts of sweets.

Mandir means temple.

Giving and sharing

Use these activities to help the children appreciate the food that they eat every day

How do you feel?

Stepping Stone: express needs and feelings in appropriate ways (PSED).
Early Learning Goal: have a developing awareness of their own needs, views and feelings and be sensitive to the needs, views and feeling of others (PSED).
Group size: up to eight children.

What you need

Selection of fruit (check for food allergies and dietary requirements); knife (adult use); plates; information books and pictures about different festivals.

What to do

● Start by talking about the significance of food during festival times. Use the information from the books and pictures as reference.
● Explain that during some festivals, such as Ramadan, people stop eating or 'fast' for a short time. This helps them to understand what it is like to be poor and hungry and to be grateful for their food.
● Tell the children that you have bought some fruit for snack time. Show them just one piece of fruit and invite everyone to watch as you cut it into four pieces.
● Now give one piece of fruit to four of the children. Is there enough to go around? Why not?
● How do the children who have not been given a piece of fruit feel? Be ready to reassure them, if they become overly concerned, and remind them that this is an unusual occurrence.

● Tell the children not to worry, as you have some more food stored away. Bring some more fruit out and invite them to suggest how you can make sure that everyone has something to eat.

Support and extension

Invite younger children to help to share out individual fruits, such as strawberries. Discuss with older children, and help them to understand, that some people never have enough food to eat.

© Jenny Tulip

Home links

● Ask parents to let their children bring in a piece of their favourite fruit to cut up and share.

We can share

Stepping Stone: demonstrate flexibility and adapt their behaviour to different events, social situations and changes in routine (PSED).
Early Learning Goal: work as part of a group or class, taking turns and sharing fairly (PSED).
Group size: whole group.

What you need

Selection of fruit (check for food allergies and dietary requirements); blunt knives; plates.

What to do

● Remind the children of the activity 'How do you feel?' (see above). Talk about how they felt when they realised there was not enough food to go around the group.

● With the children's help, divide up the fruit so that there is one piece per child. Invite one child to hand the plate of food around.
● Encourage everyone to choose just one piece of fruit from the plate, saying 'Thank you' when they have taken their piece. Explain that it is important to take just one piece, because if anyone takes more than one piece it will mean that someone else has to go without!
● When everyone has a piece of fruit, enjoy your snack together and talk about sharing food.

Support and extension

Work with smaller groups of younger children. Older children could help to cut the fruit into the correct number of pieces, counting the children in the group beforehand.

Further ideas

● Enjoy a cookery activity to make savoury pizzas or sandwiches to share with the group.

● Grow your own vegetables to cut up and share.

Louise Tellam
is a teacher and freelance writer.

Words and pictures

During October focus on the Jewish festival of Sukkot for these lively language activities

Our sukkah
Stepping Stone: begin to use talk to pretend imaginary situations (CLL).
Early Learning Goal: use language to imagine and recreate roles and experiences (CLL).
Group size: up to four children at a time.

What you need
Large cardboard cartons (electrical stores may provide large cartons that white goods are delivered in) or corrugated card; twigs (preferably with leaves attached); black fabric; stapler (adult use); silver foil; scissors; masking tape; glue; plastic fruit and vegetables; pictures of fruit and vegetables from magazines; bamboo or rush mat; information books and pictures about Sukkot.

What to do
● Tell the children about the festival of Sukkot, using the information in the books and pictures. Talk about the words associated with the festival such as sukkah, lulav and etrog.
● Explain that you would like the children's help to make a sukkah in your setting.
● Make the walls of the sukkah from corrugated card or cardboard cartons, secured to the wall with masking tape.
● Invite the children to glue pictures of fruit and vegetables to the inside walls.
● Glue silver foil stars to the black fabric. Drape it across the den, star side down, so that it forms the roof of the sukkah, then staple in place.

● Secure leafy twigs and branches on top of the black fabric.
● Place a selection of toy fruit and vegetables inside the sukkah.
● Encourage the children to play freely in the area, making up stories and role-playing scenarios. They could imagine that they are travelling across the desert and staying in a sukkah, or they could pretend that they are a family celebrating the festival of Sukkot together.

Support and extension
Sit in the den with younger children to support and encourage their ideas. Older children could draw pictures of objects and foods associated with Sukkot to attach to the sukkah walls.

© Jenny Tulip

Home links
● Ask parents for old gardening catalogues or magazines for your activities.

● Some parents may also have decorative fruits and vegetables that they can lend you for decorating the sukkah.

Tastes and textures
Stepping Stone: build up vocabulary that reflects the breadth of their experiences (CLL).
Early Learning Goal: extend their vocabulary, exploring the meaning and sounds of new words (CLL).
Group size: up to eight children.

What you need
Variety of fruit cut into snack-size pieces (check for food allergies and dietary requirements); pieces of card; black marker pen; display board; Blu-Tack.

What to do
● Remind the children that, during Sukkot, many families share meals in their sukkah.
● Sit in a circle together and explain that you are going to share some fruit.
● Invite one child to take the plate around the circle, letting every child choose one piece of fruit each.

● Encourage the children to taste the fruit, closing their eyes so that they can really concentrate on the texture, smell and taste.
● Now invite the children to describe their ideas to you. Encourage them to be as descriptive as possible – what sort of texture does the banana have? Squidgy, slimy, soft? What does the apple taste like? Tangy, sweet, crunchy?
● Write the children's descriptive words on pieces of card to make labels. Attach the labels, with Blu-Tack, alongside pictures of the relevant fruits, to a display board at the children's height.
● Return to the display over time to recap on the vocabulary, adding new words as the children suggest them.

Support and extension
Ask younger children questions to encourage their vocabulary skills. Older children could take photographs of everyone eating their fruit to make a display. (Ask for parents' permission first.)

Further ideas
● Hold your story time or song time in your sukkah.

● 'Write' and decorate invitations, inviting visitors to see your sukkah.

Lynn Huggins-Cooper is a children's author and PGCE science/DT lecturer.

Fruity poems

Stepping Stone: show awareness of rhyme and alliteration (CLL).
Early Learning Goal: hear and say initial and final sounds in words, and short vowel sounds within words (CLL).
Group size: up to six children.

What you need
Pictures and information books about Sukkot; whiteboard; black marker pen.

What to do
● Talk about the fruits that are traditionally associated with Sukkot. Explain that you are going make up a fruity poem for Sukkot!
● Start by giving an example. Say:
'I ate some delicious fruit today! A crunchy, crispy apple'.
● Invite one of the children to add the next line, for example:
'A tasty, tangy plum'.
● Each time, encourage the children to think about words that start with the same sound. Refer back to your display board of descriptive words to help them.
● As each child says adds a line to the poem, write it on the whiteboard.
● When you have finished your group poem, transcribe it on to a large piece of paper to add to your display board.

© World Religions Photo Library

Support and extension
Work with just two or three younger children at a time and make up a poem together. Help older children to write out their verse, then invite them to illustrate it before adding it to your 'fruity' display.

© Jenny Tulip

Making lists

Stepping Stone: draw and paint, sometimes giving meaning to marks; ascribe meaning to marks (CLL).
Early Learning Goal: attempt writing for different purposes, using features of different forms such as lists, stories and instructions (CLL).
Group size: whole group.

What you need
Paint; sugar paper; potatoes or sponges (cut into fruit shapes); shallow tray; plastic, play-dough fruit and vegetables; fabric; table; shopping baskets; play till; play money.

What to do
● Invite the children to use the fruit-shaped sponges or potatoes to print borders around the coloured sugar paper. More able children may be able to produce simple repeating patterns.
● While these are drying, ask the children to help you make a 'market stall'. Cover the table with fabric and arrange the pretend fruit and vegetables on the table.
● On their printed paper, invite the children to 'write' or draw what they would like to 'buy' from the stall.
● Invite one child to be the stallholder. Encourage the other children to share their lists with the stallholder, working out together what they have chosen to buy on their list and loading it into the baskets.

Support and extension
Provide 'fruit and vegetable' words to overwrite, or templates to trace, on the writing table for younger children. Invite older children to write a menu for a meal for everyone to share in their sukkah.

Festival countdown

Use these familiar festival themes as preparation for a wide range of celebrations throughout the year

All wrapped up

Stepping Stone: begin to talk about the shapes of everyday objects (MD).
Early Learning Goal: use language such as 'circle' or 'bigger' to describe the shape and size of solids and flat shapes (MD).
Group size: up to six children.

What you need

Selection of presents associated with different festivals such as an Easter egg for Easter, rakhi (or friendship bracelets) for Raksha Bandhan, new toys and books for Christmas and fortune cookies for Chinese New Year; wrapping paper; sticky tape; scissors; box.

What to do

● Talk about the different festivals that the children know about. Is it traditional to give presents at any of these festivals?
● Discusss the type of presents that the children have given and received during the festivals that they celebrate.
● Show the children your selection of presents that are linked to certain festivals.
● Invite the children to take turns to come and select a present to wrap. Ask them to describe their chosen object. Is it round or square? Is it heavy or light? Is it soft or hard? Is it big or small?

● Now help the children to wrap their present. Talk to them about the shape and size of the object.
● Place all the presents in a box and invite the children to take turns to take out a present and guess what it is by the way that it looks and feels.
● Encourage the children to unwrap their present to see if they have guessed correctly.

Support and extension

Choose gifts that are clearly different in size and shape for younger children to guess. Encourage older children to group the parcels based on certain criteria such as small, heavy, round, square and so on.

© Photodisc, Inc

Further ideas

● Make some paper decorations with symmetrical designs.

● With parental permission, take photographs of all your festival celebrations to compile into a festival yearbook. The children will enjoy looking back at them.

Fun and games

Stepping Stone: use some number names accurately in play (MD).
Early Learning Goal: say and use number names in order in familiar contexts (MD).
Group size: small groups.

What you need

Outdoor area; chalks; balls; skittles; extra adult helpers; selection of board games.

What to do

● Talk to the children about games and activities that are linked to a range of festivals, for example, paint splattering for Holi and carol singing at Christmas.
● Tell the children that you are going to have a games afternoon (possibly linked to the festival that you are currently celebrating).

● Invite extra adult helpers to join you and set up three or four traditional games that involve counting and/or number recognition, such as hopscotch, ball games that include counting the number of times the children can bounce or catch the ball without dropping it or hitting numbered skittles, and board games, such as Lotto and Snakes and ladders. Sing or act out some traditional counting rhymes (such as 'Five Currant Buns' or 'Ten Little Monkeys').
● Arrange for the children to rotate around the different games with the adults helping them to recognise and say numbers.

Support and extension

Provide lots of short, simple games for younger children and keep numbers to below five. Ask older children to make up their own games that involve counting and recognising numbers.

Home links

● Invite parents to your setting to talk to the children about any of these specific festival themes.

Sally Gray
is an early years
writer and editor.

Festival food

Stepping Stone: order two items by weight or capacity (MD).
Early Learning Goal: use language such as 'greater', 'smaller', 'heavier' or 'lighter' to compare quantities (MD).
Group size: four children.

What you need

Basic biscuit recipe and ingredients; kitchen scales; range of different-sized spoons, scoops and cups; oven; mixing bowls; aprons.

What to do

● Ask the children to tell you about any festivals that they can think of where they ate some special food.
● Make a list of the festival foods that the children know about, for example, Christmas cake, Simnel cake (Easter) and Charoset (Pesach).
● Explain that you have a recipe for biscuits that the children can help you to make whenever you are celebrating a festival or special occasion.
● Make the recipe more special by cutting out the biscuits with relevant shape cutters, such as snowmen for Christmas, or by adding icing patterns, such as rangoli patterns for Divali.
● Invite the children to help you weigh out the ingredients. Use different-sized cups, spoons and scoops to measure out the ingredients before weighing them. Ask the

children to compare the different amounts. Which cup holds the most flour? Which is the biggest spoon? How many scoops of sugar fit into this cup?
● Show the children how to weigh the ingredients accurately and then make the biscuits together.
● Decorate the biscuits to suit your current festival work.

Support and extension

Concentrate on the size differences with younger children. Encourage older children to fill all the cups with sugar or flour. Ask them to put them in order of their capacity.

© Comstock

Decorate and celebrate

Stepping Stone: show interest by sustained construction activity or by talking about shapes or arrangements (MD).
Early Learning Goal: talk about, recognise and recreate simple patterns (MD).
Group size: up to five children.

© Jenny Tulip

What you need

Pictures of a range of festival celebrations; selection of decorations; shape templates; sticky coloured paper; pencils; scissors; long strips of paper.

What to do

● Look at the pictures of the different festival celebrations. What decorations do the children notice?
● Show the children your selection of decorations. Let them look at and handle them. Talk about any shapes and patterns that they can see.
● Now give the children some shape templates and sticky coloured paper. Ask them to draw around and cut out several shapes. Put all the children's shapes together, encouraging them to describe and match the shapes as they sort them.
● Now give each child a long strip of paper and explain that they are going to make their own decorative banner using the shapes. Suggest that they place the shapes in their chosen pattern on the strip of paper before they stick them down. Encourage the children to tell you about their patterns and shapes.
● Once they are happy with their designs, let the children stick the shapes into place. Use the banners to decorate your room for a special occasion.

Support and extension

Concentrate on two or three shapes with younger children. Encourage older children to make a repeating pattern banner.

Festivals
Let's share

Use these ideas to help the children to think about kindness and sharing

Love in a box

Stepping Stone: gain an awareness of the cultures and beliefs of others (KUW).
Early Learning Goal: begin to know about their own cultures and beliefs and those of other people (KUW).
Group size: whole group.

What you need

Paper; box, decorated with colourful paper; pictures, books and video clips illustrating kindness, sharing and giving; paper; scissors; glue; colouring materials.

Preparation

Cut heart shapes from the paper, large enough for a child to stick on a picture and/or write a few words.

What to do

● Sit together in a circle. Talk about the festival of Eid-ul-Fitr explaining that, during this festival, Muslims think about sharing and giving to help others. They give money to the poor, settle squabbles or disagreements (make friends) and give gifts, sweets and cards to family and friends.
● Ask 'Has anyone done anything kind for you?', 'How did it make you feel?', 'Have you done anything kind or thoughtful for anyone else?'.
● Give each child a piece of heart-shaped paper and invite them to draw a picture of something that they could do, give or share with the other children in the group.

● Help any children who are struggling with ideas by reminding them of times they have helped another child or adult in the group.
● Pass the box around and invite the children to put their completed heart drawings into the box.
● In your circle, take out the hearts one by one and share the ideas together.
● If any children feel confident enough, let them explain their drawings to the rest of the group.

Support and extension

Younger children could tear pictures from magazines to represent their ideas. Older children could add a few words to describe their pictures.

© Jenny Tulip

Home links

● Ask parents to cook something at home with their children to bring into your setting and share with the group.

● Encourage the children to do something to help at home each day and make a diary to show to the group.

What a treat!

Stepping Stone: begin to try out a range of tools and techniques safely (KUW).
Early Learning Goal: select the tools and techniques they need to shape, assemble and join materials they are using (KUW).
Group size: four to six children.

What you need

Equipment: chopping board; plate; circle of non-stick silicone paper; sharp knife (adult use); saucepan; teaspoons; two bowls; hot water; aprons. **Ingredients:** 230g white chocolate; 230g milk chocolate; individual bowls containing glacé cherries, dried apricots, sultanas, raisins and grapes (chopped into smaller pieces).

Preparation

Check for food allergies and dietary requirements.

What to do

● Remind the children that, during Eid-ul-Fitr,

Muslims share food, sweets and presents. Invite the children to work together to prepare some tasty treats to share at home or in your setting. Ask everyone to wash their hands and put on aprons.
● Put some hot water in the saucepans and rest the bowls on top so that they sit in the hot water. Ask the children to help you break the chocolate into the bowls and stir carefully until it has melted.
● Place the silicone paper on the plate. Invite the children to take turns dropping teaspoons of white and brown melted chocolate on to the paper.
● Now encourage the children to decorate the chocolate drops, choosing the toppings that they would like from the individual bowls.
● Put in the fridge for 30 minutes, then enjoy sharing!

Support and extension

Help younger children to take turns and share. Let older children, under close supervision, help you to chop the ingredients.

Further idea

● Take the children to visit a mosque or invite a Muslim parent or visitor to talk to the children.

Martine Horvath
is a Reception teacher and early years educational consultant.

Celebrate with style

During November enjoy these exciting Divali activities and provide opportunities to develop fine and gross motor skills

Pretty patterns

Stepping Stone: manipulate materials to achieve a planned effect (PD).

Early Learning Goal: handle tools, objects, construction and malleable materials safely and with increasing control (PD).

Group size: up to ten children.

What you need

Examples of rangoli patterns (copy from books or draw your own on to A4 paper, then photocopy); glue; spreaders; resources and pictures related to Divali, including posters, music, cards, divas and videos; colouring materials including chalks, pens, crayons, paints, coloured sand and pastels.

What to do

● Enjoy sharing your Divali resources. Tell the children that you are going to make some rangoli patterns using lots of different equipment and techniques.

● Give each child a sheet of rangoli patterns. Invite the children to choose how they would like to decorate their patterns, using the materials available.

● If using sand, demonstrate how to spread glue on one section of pattern at a time and carefully sprinkle on sand using a finger and thumb pincer grip.

● If using chalk, demonstrate how to achieve a smooth effect by smudging and spreading it with your finger.

● If you have a paved outdoor area, go outside and enjoy the activity on a larger scale! Draw a faint outline in white chalk and invite the children to draw over it using coloured chalks, then fill in the outline with coloured sand. Encourage them to do this by filling beakers or pots with sand and carefully sprinkling it inside the chalked lines.

Support and extension

Provide simplified patterns for younger children to copy. Encourage older children to create their own symmetrical rangoli patterns on paper, peg boards or squared paper.

Home links

● Encourage the children to look at symmetrical patterns in homes, buildings and nature and to draw and share with the group.

© Gaynor Berry

Divali dance

Stepping Stone: experiment with different ways of moving (PD).

Early Learning Goal: move with confidence, imagination and in safety (PD).

Group size: up to ten children.

What you need

Pictures and posters depicting the Divali story; Divali cards; book such as *The Divali Small Book* by Anita Ganeri and Carole Gray (Evans Brothers); appropriate music such as *The Rough Guide to the Music of India and Pakistan* (World Music Network), (available from Religion in Evidence, freephone: 0800-318686); CD player or tape recorder.

Preparation

Invite Hindu parents, practitioners or visitors to your setting to perform a dance for the children.

What to do

● If possible, enjoy a performance from an Indian dancer, child, parent or practitioner or simply enjoy talking about the story of Divali, making good use of the posters, pictures and music.

● Ask the children what kinds of things they might do to show that they are really happy or excited about something. Some may suggest jumping for joy, smiling, shouting and dancing.

● Talk about how happiness and stories can be conveyed through dance. Emphasise this by inviting the children to sing the traditional song 'If You're Happy and You Know it'.

● Play some Indian music, and encourage the children to make up their own happy dances, either individually or in pairs.

● Invite your visitor or parents to watch the children's dances.

Support and extension

Encourage younger children to work in pairs and to watch each other for ideas. Invite older children to demonstrate and perform their dance individually or in pairs to the rest of the group.

Further ideas

● Have a 'Follow-my-leader Divali dance' where the children follow and copy their friends' dance movements.

● Make colourful bead bangles to wear for your Divali dance.

Martine Horvath
is a Reception teacher and early years educational consultant.

Crafty creations

Focus on the Hindu birthday celebration of Ganesh Chaturthi during September as you enjoy these creative play ideas

Elephant masks

Stepping Stone: make three-dimensional structures (CD).

Early Learning Goal: explore colour, texture, shape, form and space in two or three dimensions (CD).

Group size: six children.

What you need

Picture of Ganesha; balloons; clear petroleum jelly; strips of newspaper; cold-water paste; grey paint; card; scissors; sticky tape; coloured foil; sequins; grey ribbon; grey socks; fabric scraps; hole punch; pictures and information books about the festival of Ganesh Chaturthi.

What to do

● Talk about the festival of Ganesh Chaturthi using the information in the books and pictures.
● Look at a picture of Ganesha and suggest that the children make elephant masks.
● Blow up three balloons, then invite pairs of children to work together to cover each balloon with a thin layer of petroleum jelly.
● Next, cover the balloons with strips of newspaper dipped in the paste. Continue until they are covered with at least four layers of paper. Hang them up to dry.
● Cut the balloons in half and give one half to each child. Invite them to paint their masks grey.
● Let the children create trunks by stuffing grey socks with small pieces of fabric.
● Cut two eye holes and a hole in the middle of each child's mask for the trunk. Thread the open end of a stuffed grey sock through the centre hole and tape the end securely to the back of the mask.
● Cut grey ears and white tusks from card and tape them to the masks.

● Punch a hole in each side of the masks and tie a length of ribbon to each one.
● Invite the children to add headdresses to their masks, using strips of card decorated with coloured foil and sequins.
● Secure the ribbons around the children's heads and let them enjoy wearing their elephant masks.

Support and extension

Help younger children to create paper-plate masks instead. Challenge older children to make trunks by folding strips of grey paper into zigzags.

© TRIP/H Rogers

The dance of the elephant

Stepping Stone: try to capture experiences and responses with music and dance (CD).

Early Learning Goal: respond in a variety of ways to what they see and hear (CD).

Group size: up to ten children.

What you need

Elephant masks from 'Elephant masks' activity (see above); grey fabric; grey ribbon; thread; scissors; CD or tape recording of *The Carnival of the Animals* by Saint-Saëns; tape recorder or CD player.

What to do

● Create simple tabards from grey fabric by cutting out a large rectangle, twice the length of the average child from neck to knee. Cut a hole for the child's head in the centre and sew ribbon fastenings to the sides.
● Listen to the 'Elephant movement' from *The Carnival of the Animals* and talk about how elephants move.
● Suggest that the children wear their masks and tabards as they pretend to be elephants plodding around the room to the music.

Support and extension

Younger children may move more comfortably without wearing masks. Suggest that older children make up stories about elephants using the masks and tabards.

Home links

● Send home instructions for making animal masks.

● Invite parents to watch their children dance in their costumes.

Further ideas

● Create masks for other festivals using the same method.

● Introduce small-world elephants into sand and water play.

Jean Evans is an early years consultant and author.

Chapter 6
Under the sea

Journey deep beneath the waves and find out about the animals and plants that inhabit our seas with the exciting ideas in this chapter. From fantasy mermaids to ferocious sharks these activities will encourage children to use their imaginative skills to the full as they find out about our undersea world.

Sea life spectacular!

Use the natural wonders of the sea to bring together an exciting array of sea life inspired language and literacy activities

Penguin party

Stepping Stone: have emerging self-confidence to speak to others (CLL).
Early Learning Goal: interact with others, negotiating plans and activities (CLL).
Group size: six children.

What you need

Sliced wholemeal bread; margarine; tinned tuna; cheese slices; tomato; thin carrot sticks; iceberg lettuce; children's cutlery; plates and bowls; apples; bananas; tinned pineapple and satsumas; blue and green sponge-painting equipment; sheets of paper.

© Corel

What to do

● Check for food allergies and dietary requirements.
● Invite the children to sponge-paint the paper to make place mats.
● While these are drying, ask the children to wash their hands thoroughly, then prepare the party food.
● Tear the lettuce to make seaweed and place a little on each plate. Help each child to cut fish shapes from the sliced cheese and add a tiny piece of tomato for an eye. Make tuna sandwiches and cut carefully into triangles. Create a simple crab, using the sandwich for the body, and adding carrot sticks for the legs and pincers.
● Wash and peel the fruit and arrange on a serving plate in the shape of a giant octopus or other choice of sea creature.
● Adapt the familiar song 'One Elephant Went Out to Play' (from *This Little Puffin* compiled by Elizabeth Matterson, Puffin Books) to sing 'One little penguin went out to play, upon an icey floe one day, he had such enormous fun, that he called for… (choose a different sea creature) to come', and so on.
● Play the game and share the party food together.

Support and extension

Younger children may need help with the cutlery. Encourage older children to make name cards to add to each place mat.

Home links

● Ask parents to join in the penguin party.

● Invite parents to bring in diving or fishing gear to show to the children.

Further ideas

● Read *Meg at Sea* by Helen Nicoll and Jan Pienkowski (Puffin Books) and make your own sea creature magic spell.

● Visit a tropical fish shop and talk about the colours and shapes of the different fish.

Mermaid's muddle

Stepping Stone: begin to use anticlockwise movement and retrace vertical lines (CLL).
Early Learning Goal: use a pencil and hold it effectively to form recognisable letters (CLL).
Group size: four children.

What you need

Illustrations of mermaids; large sheet of paper; pens; glitter; foil and other shiny collage materials; glue; thin card; scissors; small pieces of green and blue coloured paper; coloured pens and pencils.

What to do

● Draw the outline of a mermaid on the paper. Encourage the children to decorate the top half of the mermaid with collage materials.
● Make a card template for scales for the mermaid's tail. Help the children to draw around this, then cut scales from the blue and green paper, and from the foil.
● Decorate the green scales with vertical lines in sea colours. Talk about up and down movements. Encourage each child to hold their pen effectively and to steady the paper with their other hand.
● Next, sort all the blue scales and decorate with circles, curves and spirals made in an anticlockwise direction. Watch the children carefully and help them to move their pens in the correct direction.
● Finally, decorate the foil scales carefully, using a pencil to make a variety of marks and patterns. Glue the scales in place to complete the mermaid.

Support and extension

For younger children, use large brushes and green and blue paint for up and down mark-making. Let older children make repeating patterns of marks on the scales, varying the size and shapes.

Clare Beswick
is an early years and childcare consultant.

Treasure basket

Stepping Stone: hear and say the initial sound in words (CLL).
Early Learning Goal: hear and say initial and final letter sounds in words (CLL).
Group size: six children.

What you need
Pictures of sea creatures; toy sea animals; sea shells; sand in a plastic bottle; pebbles; basket or bag.

What to do
● Put the pictures and objects into the bag. Sit on the floor with the children and explain that you are going to row out to sea to see what you can find.
● Help the children to sit one behind another, with each child's legs stretched out either side of the child in front. Row the boat, swaying forwards and backwards slowly in a rowing action.
● Next, gradually pull the basket towards you. Invite a child to choose an object from the basket, keeping their choice hidden from the other children. Ask them to describe the object and to name the first letter sound. Prompt with simple questions.
● Continue to explore the basket of sea-life objects, with each child in turn choosing, describing and identifying the initial letter sound.

Support and extension
Work with three younger children and use just three objects in the bag. Return each object to the bag, allowing for repetition. Write down the letter sounds for older children. Encourage them to name the final letter sounds, too.

© Digital Vision Ltd

Rock-pool water play

Stepping Stone: use a widening range of words to express or elaborate ideas (CLL).
Early Learning Goal: speak clearly and audibly with confidence and control and show awareness of the listener (CLL).
Group size: four children.

What you need
Shallow plastic trays; small-world people; strips of green and blue Cellophane or plastic aquarium plants; pebbles and sea shells; tea strainers as nets; sand; water; plastic sea creatures.

What to do
● Cover the base of each tray with a thin layer of sand, add water and allow the sand to settle.
● Add the other items to create a rock-pool play scene.
● Use open questions and comments as you play alongside the children. Help them to elaborate their ideas and encourage them to add other appropriate items to extend their play.

Support and extension
Model simple pretend play for younger children. Help older children to find pictures of the sea creatures in a rock pool.

© Angela Lambert/ Beehive Illustration

Under the sea

All at sea

Focus on shapes and numbers with these fun maths activities

Shells!

Stepping Stone: show curiosity and observation by talking about shapes, how they are the same or why some are different (MD).
Early Learning Goal: use developing mathematical ideas and methods to solve practical problems (MD).
Group size: small groups.

What you need
Shells of various shapes, sizes, colours and textures from existing collections; transparent tubs; backing paper; display board; white paper; pens.

What to do
● Examine the shells together. How many words can the children can think of to describe them (rough, hard, bumpy)?
● Invite the children to discuss the many ways in which the shells can be sorted.
● Provide transparent tubs and ask the children to sort the shells first by colour, then by shape, size and texture.
● Demonstrate how to arrange the shells in a line from smallest to largest and use vocabulary such as 'smaller', 'larger', 'smallest', 'same'.
● Using the mathematical concepts you have explored, make a large display.
● Stick the shells on to backing paper in groups and invite the children to write accompanying labels.

© Corel

Support and extension
Limit the number of shells that you use for younger children. Suggest that older children weigh the shells using simple weighing scales. Encourage them to find out which shell is the heaviest and which is the lightest, then line them up in the correct order.

Favourite sea creatures

Stepping Stone: show an interest in numbers and counting (MD).
Early Learning Goal: say and use number names in order in familiar contexts (MD).
Group size: whole group.

What you need
Large sheets of paper; marker pen.

What to do
● Ask the children to name as many sea creatures as they can. Write them on a large sheet of paper.
● Discuss the characteristics of each creature. How many eyes does each have? How many legs? How do they move around?
● Have a vote on which creature the children like the best. Explain that each child is only allowed to have one vote.
● Draw a simple picture of each sea creature on the large sheet of paper and make a tally chart of the votes next to each.
● Discuss your findings. Which creature was the most popular? Which was the least?

Support and extension
Invite younger children to decorate the tally chart with drawings of the sea creatures that they have discussed, using picture books as a guide. Encourage older children to experiment with other types of graphs, such as simple bar charts or pictographs.

Home links
● Let parents borrow the laminated fish and shark cards and encourage them to play the game at home with their children.

● Encourage parents to take their children to a local library to find books about sea creatures.

Further ideas
● Hide some shells in the sand tray and invite the children to hunt them out. Set a time limit and see who can find the most shells.

● Put some shells in a large transparent jar and ask the children to estimate how many are inside.

● Peg the fish and shark cards in a reccurring pattern on a washing line or display board.

● Sing the song 'One, Two, Three, Four, Five, Once I Caught a Fish Alive' using fish cards as counting props.

Allison Hedley is a nursery nurse and Degree student at Sunderland University.

Shark!

Stepping Stone: match some shapes by recognising similarities and orientation (MD).
Early Learning Goal: talk about, recognise and recreate simple patterns
Group size: two to four children (MD).

What you need

Thin card; A4 paper; scissors; laminating materials.

Preparation

Divide a sheet of A4 paper into six sections. Draw five fish outlines and one shark outline in the six sections. Make six photocopies on to thin card, then cut into individual cards.

What to do

● Discuss the concept of the game of 'Snap!' with the children.
● Explain that in this game, the children take turns to turn over a card, one at a time. Once the card is turned over, the children must say what they see, for example, 'fish'.
● Before you begin to play the game, hide some shark cards in among the fish. Each time a shark is turned over the first child to shout 'Shark!' can keep all the cards that have been turned over. Tell the children that they are going to have to watch very

carefully to spot the shape of the shark among the fish!
● Find out who has the most fish and who has the most sharks.

Support and extension

Limit the number of cards for younger children. Challenge older children to see if they can pair up matching fish shapes.

Counting octopus

Stepping Stone: show increased confidence with numbers by spotting errors (MD).
Early Learning Goal: recognise numerals 1 to 9 (MD).
Group size: small groups.

What you need

Balloon; black marker pen; old clean tights; old newspapers; sticky dots; sticky tape.

What to do

● Construct a large group octopus by blowing up a balloon for the head and drawing on the facial features using a black marker pen. Invite the children to scrunch up old newspapers and stuff them into the legs of the old tights to make eight individual tentacles.
● Write the numerals 1 to 8 around the bottom of the balloon.
● Ask the children to help you to stick a corresponding number of spots to each tentacle, so that you have one spot on one leg, two on the next and so on.
● Mix all the tentacles into a pile. Invite individual children to choose a tentacle and stick it on to the octopus next to the correct number.
● Check each tentacle as it is stuck on and invite the other children to say whether it is in the correct place or not.

Support and extension

Limit the number of tentacles used for younger children. Encourage older children to choose two random tentacles and add the numbers together, then let them experiment with subtraction.

Fishy friends

Encourage the children to think about sharing with others using these activities based on a favourite book

Scale by scale

Stepping Stone: seek out others to share experiences (PSED).
Early Learning Goal: work as part of a group, taking turns and sharing fairly (PSED).
Group size: small group.

What you need

The Rainbow Fish by Marcus Pfister (North-South Books); large outline shape of the Rainbow Fish; scale shapes pre-cut from card; paint in various colours; paintbrushes; shiny paper; glue; scissors.

What to do

● Read the story of *The Rainbow Fish* to the children. Explain that you are going to make a giant collage of the fish.
● Ask each child to work on one scale and choose a colour to paint it.
● Work together to make the Rainbow Fish's last shiny scale. Each child can take turns to glue on some shiny paper.
● When all the scales are finished, help the children to decide how to arrange them on the fish. Where will they place the shiny scale?
● Label the individual scales with the children's names. Display the Rainbow Fish on the wall to remind the children about sharing.

© Angela Lambert/ Beehive Illustration

Support and extension

Help younger children to recognise their name and scribe it on their scale. Let older children write their own names. Invite older children to paint some of the other fish from the story. Remember to give each fish just one shiny scale.

Home links

● Encourage parents to talk with their children about sharing with friends and siblings.

● Organise a special 'Sharing Day'. Ask children to bring in toys from home to share with their friends.

Pass the fish

Stepping Stone: begin to accept the needs of others, with support (PSED).
Early Learning Goal: consider the consequences of their words and actions for themselves and others (PSED).
Group size: whole group.

What you need

The Rainbow Fish by Marcus Pfister (North-South Books); toy fish (a hand-puppet Rainbow Fish is available from Puppets by Post, tel: 01462-446040); biscuits or other food to share (check for food allergies and dietary requirements).

What to do

● Read the story of *The Rainbow Fish* up to 'Now he was the loneliest fish in the entire ocean'. Talk about how the little blue fish felt when the Rainbow Fish would not give him one shiny scale. Why was the Rainbow Fish lonely? What do the children think the Rainbow Fish should have done?

● Read the rest of the story. Did the Rainbow Fish do what the children expected? Was he still lonely at the end of the story?
● Sit in a circle together. Pass the toy fish around as you sing this song to the tune of 'Frère Jacques'.

We are sharing, we are sharing,
With our friends, with our friends,
Sharing makes us happy, sharing makes us happy.
It's good to share, it shows we care.

● Invite the child who is holding the fish at the end of the song to discuss how they feel if someone does not share a toy with them. Is it easy to share a special toy with the other children?
● At the end of the session, share some food together. Ask one child who usually finds it hard to share to hand out the biscuits.

Support and extension

Act out *The Rainbow Fish* to reinforce the sharing message for younger children. Encourage older children to relate and role-play their own experiences of sharing or not sharing to the group.

Further idea

● Make badges saying 'I can share' with a small, shiny scale on, to remind the children of the Rainbow Fish.

Judith Harries
is an early years teacher and writer.

Underwater world

Journey beneath the waves with these exciting activities

Yellow submarine

Stepping Stone: construct with a purpose in mind, using a variety of resources (KUW).
Early Learning Goal: build and construct with a wide range of objects, selecting appropriate resources, and adapting their work where necessary (KUW).
Group size: up to five children.

What you need
Litre-sized plastic bottles; yellow paper (preferably sticky); yellow card; kitchen roll tubes; scissors; sticky tape; glue sticks; black marker pens; a recording of the song *Yellow Submarine* (available from Early Learning Centre); tape recorder; pictures of submarines.

What to do
● Listen to the song *Yellow Submarine* and find out what the children know about submarines.
● Look at the pictures of the submarines. Tell the children that they are all going to make a submarine. Give each child a plastic bottle and cover it with yellow paper.
● Decide together what else needs to be added. Help the children to cut out pieces of card to make 'wings' and other shapes.
● Show the children how to cut slits in the base of a section of a kitchen-roll tube in order to fan it out and fix it to the surface of the covered bottle to make a 'conning tower'.
● Demonstrate to the children how to attach a piece of card to the base of the 'submarine' to stop it moving around. Finish the submarines by drawing windows and other adornments using a thick black marker pen.

© Digital Vision Ltd

Support and extension
Pre-cut all the necessary shapes for younger children and simply help them to fix them together. Let older children experiment with different ways of fixing the submarine together.

Home links
● Make some underwater creature templates for the children to take home. Ask parents to help their children to use them to make underwater pictures together. Encourage the children to bring in their pictures to share with the rest of the group.

Further ideas
● Provide some underwater dressing-up clothes, such as masks, snorkels, swimhats, flippers and wetsuits, for the children to play with.

● Provide an assortment of different-coloured and different-textured paper, and use a range of cutting techniques, such as tearing, cutting and crimping, to create some underwater creatures.

Under the sea

Stepping Stone: show curiosity, observe and manipulate objects (KUW).
Early Learning Goal: find out about, and identify, some features of living things, objects and events they observe (KUW).
Group size: up to four children.

What you need
Books showing underwater environments; water tray and water; washed sand and gravel; pebbles; plastic sea creatures; Plasticine; plastic weeds.

What to do
● Look at the pictures of underwater environments together. Talk about the different sea creatures in the pictures and consider what they might like to eat and where they take shelter.
● Put a shallow amount of water in the water tray. Explain to the children that they are going to make an underwater world for your plastic sea creatures. (If some of them float, stick them into pieces of Plasticine to weigh them down.)
● Invite the children to add pebbles, sand, gravel and weeds to the tray. Encourage them to talk about the underwater 'world' and the sea creatures' needs as they work.

Support and extension
Make a mock-up tray for younger children to look at and copy. Encourage older children to learn and use the names of the sea creatures in the tray.

Sally Gray
is an early years
writer and editor.

Under the waves

Use a parachute to recreate the motion of the water with these exciting movement ideas

Making waves

Stepping Stone: respond to rhythm, music and story, by means of gesture and movement (PD).
Early Learning Goal: move with confidence, imagination and in safety (PD).
Group size: whole group or small groups, depending on the size of your parachute.

What you need

A parachute or similar-sized piece of lightweight fabric; selection of pictures showing calm and stormy seas; music to represent calm and stormy seas (SpaceKraft supplies suitable music tapes, tel: 01274-581007 for a catalogue); tape recorder.

What to do

● Show the children the pictures of the sea and encourage them to describe how the sea looks. Is it flat, still, wavy? Do they think it is a sunny day or a windy day?
● Next, invite the children to close their eyes and play the pieces of sea music to them.
● Which piece of music do they think best matches the calm sea picture and the stormy sea picture?
● Sit the children around the parachute. Ask them to hold on to the parachute and to gently shake it

© Angela Lambert

to create waves. Encourage them to practise shaking it very gently to create the sea on a calm day, then shake it more vigorously to create a stormy sea.
● When they are confident doing this, play the music and encourage them to shake the parachute to match the music.

Support and extension

For younger children, or those who have not used a parachute before, sit them next to an adult who can offer help and assistance in moving and controlling the parachute. Older children could lead the activity by taking it in turns to call out 'calm sea', 'stormy sea', 'windy day', 'sunny day' and so on.

Sea creatures swim

Stepping Stones: move in a range of ways; adjust speed or change direction to avoid obstacles (PD).
Early Learning Goal: move with confidence, imagination and in safety (PD).
Group size: whole group or small groups, depending on the size of your parachute.

What you need

A parachute or similar-sized piece of lightweight fabric; six pictures of different sea creatures mounted on to individual pieces of card.

What to do

● Discuss with the children the types of creatures that are found in the sea.
● Show the children the picture cards. Ask them how each creature might move in the water.
● Sit together around the parachute and give each child a picture card.

● Explain to the children that they need to listen carefully to the instructions that you are going to give them. Some instructions will be for the whole group, some will be for just one creature.
● When you say 'Sea creatures swim', lift the parachute in the air, while all the children swim underneath it, pretending to be the creatures on their card. When you say individual creatures, for example, 'fishes swim' or 'whales swim', only the children holding those cards should swim underneath the parachute.
● Try other commands such as 'Sea creatures rest' (place the parachute on the floor while the children sit around the edge); 'Calm seas' (children swim slowly) and 'Stormy seas' (children swim quickly).

Support and extension

To keep it simple, use fewer instructions for younger children. Invite older children to suggest their own instructions. They could also take it in turns to call out the instructions to the others.

Home links

● Suggest that when the children have a bath at home, they add boats and practise making calm and stormy seas for them to sail on.

Further ideas

● Invite a group of children to play a selection of musical instruments, quietly for calm seas and loudly for stormy seas, while another group moves the parachute in time to the sounds made.

● Tell a story about a boat on the sea with plenty of descriptions of how the sea is moving. Encourage the children to move the parachute in response to the story.

Jenny Etheredge
is the Pre-School Leader at Thames Pre-School in Cricklade, Wiltshire.

Seaside showtime

Have fun making some undersea creatures for this shimmering shadow play!

Silly octopus!

Stepping Stone: make three-dimensional structures (CD).

Early Learning Goal: explore colour, texture, shape, form and space in two or three dimensions (CD).

Group size: small groups.

What you need

For each child: circle of green felt (approximately dinner-plate size), black felt, old tennis ball, elastic band, scissors, shirring elastic, two lolly sticks; needle and thread (adult use); glue; pictures of octopuses.

What to do

● Ask the children if they know what an octopus is. Where do they live? What do they look like? Has anyone ever seen an octopus? Use pictures to enhance your discussion.
● Give each child a tennis ball and circle of green felt. Demonstrate to the children how to wrap the felt around the tennis ball and secure it with an elastic band.
● Invite the children to cut out eight legs, eyes and a mouth from the black felt, and to glue them on to the octopus.
● Cut nine lengths of shirring elastic, each 15cm long. Knot the end of each piece of elastic and thread one through the end of each leg.

● Glue or tie two lolly sticks together to make a cross. Tie the shirring elastic of two legs together and attach them to the lolly sticks. Sew a length of elastic to the octopus' head and tie it around the middle of the lolly sticks. You now have a silly octopus puppet! If possible, let the children watch video footage of real octopuses and observe how they move in the sea.
● Let the children experiment with moving their puppets in different ways.

© Angela Lambert/Beehive Illustration

Support and extension

Encourage younger children to group together and create a shared octopus. Invite older children to make individual octopuses.

Undersea shadows

Stepping Stone: use available resources to create props to support role play (CD).

Early Learning Goal: use their imagination in art and design, music, dance, imaginative and role play and stories (CD).

Group size: large group.

What you need

Picture books containing sea creatures; large blue sheet; overhead projector; cardboard; scissors; craft materials; thick, black marker pen; long sticks or garden canes.

What to do

● Look at the picture books and discuss the different sea creatures. Talk about their features such as eyes, scales, flippers and fins.
● Using a thick, black marker pen, draw simple templates of each sea creature and cut them out.
● Give each child a sea creature template and

invite them to decorate it using the craft materials provided. Encourage them to pay attention to the features that you discussed, referring to the picture books for guidance.
● Attach each sea creature to a long stick or a length of garden cane.
● Ask four children to hold up the blue sheet. Switch on the overhead projector and turn the room lights off.
● Invite the other children to create shadows with their creatures to make them look as if they are swimming through the blue sea. Experiment with different ways of twisting and turning, ducking and diving.
● Remember to use your silly octopus puppet from the activity above!

Support and extension

Guide younger children with a helping hand. Invite older children to create a simple play with characters and a story.

Further ideas

● Cut up on old bath mat with suction cups and use them as 'octopus tentacles' on the sensory table.

● Switch on an electric fan so that the bed sheet shimmers like waves.

● Dip bubble-wrap into paint and use it to print scales on to your sea creatures.

Allison Hedley
is a nursery nurse and Degree student at Sunderland University.